Where Is God in Fearful Times?

Encouragement from Exodus

Wes Taber
Life in Messiah Global Ambassador

ISBN: 978-1-878678-10-2
Printed in the United States of America

Dedication

To Lori, my wife, who has shared the adventures of life (and LIFE) along this singularly blessed journey on which the Lord has taken us. Thank you for your patience, encouragement, and multiplied sacrifices over these "first 49" years of our marriage. The lessons reflected in this volume, and so many others, are ones we learned together. How I thank God for giving me the companion who suits me perfectly (Genesis 2:20–24)!

Soli Deo gloria.
לאדני הכבוד בלבד
To God Alone Be the Glory

Table of Contents

Foreword

When life's troubles and tragedies overwhelm us, it's easy to become fearful, despondent, and paralyzed by anxiety. On a spiritual level, we can even start questioning whether God cares about our needs as we ask ourselves, "Where is God in these fearful times of life?"

Thankfully, Wes Taber provides a reliable answer to that question by taking us on a journey into the book of Exodus. By focusing on the story of Israel's deliverance from Egypt, Wes touches on the struggles encountered by each group in this divine drama.

Like an experienced guide, Wes points out key details that highlight the circumstances faced by the different participants, and the ways God interacted with them to reveal Himself. Through his retelling of the events in Exodus 1–15, Wes helps you experience the emotional highs and lows faced by Moses, the Israelites, Pharaoh, and the Egyptians.

You will come away from *Where Is God in Fearful Times?* with new insights into the story of the Exodus. But more importantly, you will undergo a fresh encounter with the God of Abraham, Isaac, and Jacob who is still there to meet your needs in whatever fearful times of life you face today.

Dr. Charlie Dyer
Professor-at-large of Bible, Moody Bible Institute
Host, *The Land and the Book* radio program

Introduction

"God, where are You?"

Crying out to the unseen Creator of the Universe has been a common human experience throughout history. Loneliness, uncertainty, or doubt may stimulate a call heavenward. Tragedy, turmoil, or terror wring a more urgent plea from helpless souls.

The story of the Exodus is fertile soil for examining God's dealing with His people. Moses provides enough detail in his narration to allow readers to relate to the biblical characters.

Entire books have been written to give insight into this rich text. We narrow our focus here to the first 15 chapters of Exodus (through the crossing of the Red Sea). Our purpose is to examine 1) the circumstance of the main characters; 2) how God shows up (or seemingly doesn't); and 3) the effects of His presence or perceived absence.

Our hope is that you will gain wisdom in applying truths gleaned from these brief studies to your present circumstances. Finding true shalom in real life is possible when we recognize the nature and character of our sovereign, loving God.

See **insearchofshalom.com/all/storiesofshalom**

Or scan this:

Chapter 1

A Reversal of Fortune

Exodus 1:1–14

Moses begins by reminding his readers how the previous book of Genesis ended. Jacob with his 11 sons and their families, 70 persons in all, had gone down to Egypt because of famine in Canaan. Joseph was already in Egypt, and in fact had been elevated to a seat of authority second only to Pharaoh himself. The Hebrews were preserved, given pleasant dwelling space in Goshen, and they prospered.

- Genesis 49 records the death of Jacob, whose remains are brought by his sons back to the family burial ground which Abraham had purchased in Machpelah.

- Genesis 50 ends with Joseph 1) forgiving his brothers for selling him into slavery; 2) promising God would continue to care for the family and eventually return them to Canaan; then 3) dying at age 110.

The book of Exodus picks up the story with all of Joseph's brothers having died. *"But the sons of Israel were fruitful and increased greatly, and multiplied, and became exceedingly mighty, so that the land was filled with them"* (1:7).

Fear factor/Misery index:

So far, everything looks great!

The shift (Exodus 1:8–14):

A new king has arisen in Egypt – one who has no memory of the substantial blessing Joseph was to the Egyptians. This pharaoh views the prospering sons of Israel as *"more and mightier than we."* He fears they might become allies of invading enemies or move from Egypt and no longer contribute to the economy. Pharaoh sets taskmasters over the Israelites, afflicting them with hard labor as they build his storage cities of Pithom and Raamses.

"But the more [the Egyptians] afflicted them, the more they multiplied and the more they spread out, so that they were in dread of the sons of Israel" (1:12). The Egyptians' fear causes them to deal even more harshly with Jacob's offspring, embittering their lives with hard labor both in construction and agriculture.

The needle has shifted – big-time! The children of Israel have gone from blossoming to bondage, in relatively short order.

Where is God?

As Exodus begins, we have plummeted from the pinnacle of Joseph in power, with his extended family privileged, to a generation of Israelites in bondage and servitude – a very drastic change of fortunes. To this point in the story, God's name is not mentioned, though the "Joseph story" brings to mind the power of God in preserving and providing for the Jewish people in the patriarchal period.

Chapter 2
A Testimony of Faith

Exodus 1:15–22

Despite the king's efforts to subdue the Hebrew people he has enslaved, they continue to multiply. More drastic measures are called for. Of all the remedies a powerful dictator has available, which will he choose?

Shockingly – infanticide.

Pharaoh commands the Hebrew midwives, Shiphrah and Puah,[1] to murder every male child. Only girl Jewish babies are allowed to live.

The midwives' response (1:17–19):

> *"But the midwives feared God, and did not do as the king of Egypt had commanded them, but let the boys live"* (1:17).

---

1 It's sad, really, that Shiphrah and Puah seem like strange names to most people today. One would think that many families would want to name their daughters after these God-fearing, pagan king–defying heroes of the faith.

When called on the carpet for not fulfilling the king's command, Shiphrah and Puah simply "blame" it on the "vigorous" Hebrew women who deliver their babies before the midwives arrive.

Fear factor/Misery index:

Oppressively hard labor is miserable enough. But with all boy babies under threat of extinction, the future of God's chosen people seems to hang in the balance. The fear factor for Jewish families approaches the highest level as infant males are under the sentence of death.

Where is God?

For the first time in our narrative God's name has been invoked: *"the midwives feared God"* (v. 17). And the narrator comments in verse 20, *"So God was good to the midwives."*

The result? The Hebrews multiply and become very mighty! God also establishes households for the midwives who feared Him.

"Praise the LORD![2] Great story!" we might say.

And then, happily ever after?

---

2 "LORD" is the "tetragrammaton" (transliterated YHVH), the Creator's four-consonant personal name denoted by upper case letters. Alternately, "Lord" is Adonai in Hebrew; "God" is Elohim. In keeping with the command to "not take the name of the LORD your God in vain," YHVH is never pronounced. Often names of deity are not spelled out in non-sacred texts by observant Jewish people. Substitutes include names such as HaShem (literally, "the Name") or Elokim. And when the Torah is read aloud in synagogues, Adonai is vocalized wherever YHVH is written.

Our story is only beginning. And the wicked king has not given up on his evil schemes.

> *"Then Pharaoh commanded all his people, saying, 'Every son who is born you are to cast into the Nile, and every daughter you are to keep alive'"* (1:22).

His plan to have the midwives kill the Hebrews' male offspring did not succeed. But now all in Egypt are authorized by royal edict to murder Israelite baby boys.

Often life's circumstances go from bad to worse. It is natural in such times to wonder why God has not delivered us by now. "Trust in the LORD with all your heart and do not lean on your own understanding. In all your ways acknowledge Him, and He will make your paths straight" (Proverbs 3:5–6) is good counsel "for such a time as this."

Chapter 3
A Baby Boy Is Spared

It's a very familiar story – "boy meets girl" and they marry. In this instance, the writer of the story provides us with the details that both groom and bride are from the tribe of Levi. But at this point these characters are unnamed[1] – a bit unusual in a book that begins *"These are the names …"*[2]

The wife conceives and bears a son. Happy news!

Except … Hebrew baby boys are under a death sentence, remember?[3]

---

1 Amram and Jochebed are named as Moses' and Aaron's parents in Exodus 6:20.

2 In Hebrew, the Second Book of Moses is called "Shemot" ("Names"), taken from the opening sentence. The English title "Exodus" is from the Septuagint (Greek translation), meaning "the road out." The 12 sons of Israel are named in Exodus 1, as are the Hebrew midwives, Shiphrah and Puah.

3 "Every son who is born you are to cast into the Nile" was Pharaoh's edict in Exodus 1:22.

But this mom's nurturing instincts prevail. She hides her beautiful baby for three months. And then, no doubt fearful of the implications should her defiant act be discovered, she places her infant son in a pitch-sealed wicker basket among the reeds on the bank of the Nile. Her daughter[4] is strategically placed as an unobtrusive guardian.

The turn of events (Exodus 2:5–10):

The king's daughter (again, unnamed) goes to the Nile with her maidens to bathe. She spies the basket and has her maid fetch it. Opening it, she finds a crying baby boy.

The text records that *"she had pity on him and said, 'This is one of the Hebrews' children'"* (2:6).

On such a small word, "pity," hangs the fate of this infant. Surely Pharaoh's daughter knew her father's edict and what happened to those who dared disobey.

The sister of the rescued infant approaches with an offer. *"Shall I go and call a nurse for you from the Hebrew women that she may nurse the child for you?"* (2:7).

Pharaoh's daughter consents. The mother is instructed to nurse her own little boy – for pay, even! After he is weaned, Pharaoh's daughter claims him as her own. And gives him the name Moses.[5]

---

4 We learn later the elder sister's name is Miriam.

5 The English name "Moses" comes from "Moshe," which in Hebrew means "drawn out."

Fear factor/Misery index:

The focus of the story has narrowed. The majority of the Hebrews continue to suffer, both in rigorous physical labor and psychic pain as infant boys are under threat for their lives. But for one family, there is delight in the preservation of a helpless little boy, giving him a hopeful future – even if it is within the walls of the palace of a wicked and cruel king.

Where is God?

Though not explicitly mentioned in the text, we still can see evidence of the hand of the seemingly silent Almighty. How many Hebrew mothers took steps to hide their infant sons? We aren't told. We only learn of one boy who is "fished out of the Nile" by a princess.

That Jochebed has the joy of caring for her son until weaned is an unexpected blessing in the midst of a time of deep suffering. Heaven overrules the mandates of a powerful potentate once again, simply by arranging the "chance encounter" of Pharaoh's daughter with baby Moses and filling her heart with pity.

Chapter 4
"What's My Motivation Here?"

"Now it came about in those days, when Moses had grown up"[1] (2:11a) is the author's way of hitting the "fast-forward" button in our story.

Time is relative. "Time flies when you're having fun," but minutes seem like hours when burdens are crushing.

What was it like for a young Hebrew boy to be raised as a prince of Egypt? We'd have to watch a Hollywood movie to get details added by a scriptwriter because Moses provides none in the Exodus narrative. We're left to our imaginations to fill in the blanks as to what he experienced in daily life. We may safely assume Moses was in a favored position, enjoying the privileges of

---

1 Rabbinic sources posit varying ages of Moses at this point, including 40, with which Stephen concurs (Acts 7:23).

the palace and whatever education[2] a prince would be afforded.

A life-altering choice: Exodus 2:11–14

With no explanation of motivation for Moses' "field trip," verse 11 continues, *"that he went out to his brethren and looked on their hard labors."*

Whatever the rigors of his life of privilege may have entailed, they would not compare to what the oppressed Hebrews were enduring. The text is silent on what contact Moses may have maintained with his biological family, if any. How often had he made the trip to Goshen to check on how his kinsmen were faring? We do not know.[3]

"And he saw an Egyptian beating a Hebrew, one of his brethren" (2:11b). This is the second time in the verse the word "brothers" is used. In how many ways could Moses' life in the Egyptian capital be contrasted with the Hebrews? Culture, language, socio-economic status, and religion would have been markedly different. Doubtless in Egyptian society the Jewish people would be deemed inferior. Who esteems slaves?

And yet, even with all the benefits of his royal status and four decades of enculturation, Moses finds himself drawn to check on the welfare of his kin. The scene before him is of a degraded people amidst their forced labor.

---

2 Stephen notes, *"Moses was educated in all the learning of the Egyptians, and he was a man of power in words and deeds"* (Acts 7:22).

3 *"... it entered his mind to visit his brethren"* (Acts 7:23) is Stephen's interesting description. Could this have been the first time Moses entertained that thought? (And who put the idea in his head? one might wonder.)

However commonplace such violence may have been among the Hebrews, beholding the physical abuse of a kinsman hit Moses "right in the kishkes,"[4] provoking a physical response. *"So he looked this way and that, and when he saw there was no one around, he struck down the Egyptian and hid him in the sand"* (2:12).

We may imagine other options a prince may have had. Certainly, he would be accustomed to having authority in many situations. But Moses is not in Goshen in an official capacity. In fact, it appears he visits on his own, perhaps clandestinely and for the first time. Our text doesn't say.

Nor are we given any direct statement on Moses' motivation – and it's never right to presume we know the thoughts of others. Here's what we do know from the text:

1) Moses sees an Egyptian "striking/beating" a Hebrew.

2) He "turns this way and that" and sees no one.

3) He strikes/beats the Egyptian, then hides the corpse.

Why does Moses look all around? Was he seeing if anyone else would intervene? Or checking if anyone would observe his actions?

Does Moses intend to beat the Egyptian to death out of anger – or perhaps just teach him a harsh lesson, enforce justice, and defend a helpless man being beaten? Our

---

4 *Kishkes* is a Yiddish word akin to "intestines"; Moses got a gut-punch when observing the Hebrews' awful conditions.

narrator provides no insights into Moses' motivation.[5] But we are told Moses "hides" the corpse, burying in the sand the Egyptian he has killed, an indication his deed needed to be covered.

Here's what happens next:

> *13 He went out the next day, and behold, two Hebrews were fighting with each other; and he said to the offender, "Why are you striking your companion?" 14 But he said, "Who made you a prince or a judge over us? Are you intending to kill[6] me as you killed the Egyptian?" Then Moses was afraid and said, "Surely the matter has become known"* (2:13–14).

Fear factor/Misery index:

The lot of the Jewish people has not improved. In fact, in addition to servitude we are given to understand how tenuous their very existence is.

On the other hand, we find Moses traveling alone to Goshen to observe the plight of his people. In an instant, his action dramatically wrenches the course of his life. His own taking of a life had been observed – and the fear of that discovery washed over him.

---

5 Stephen provides details beyond what we learn in Exodus. *"And when [Moses] saw one of them being treated unjustly, he defended him and took vengeance for the oppressed by striking down the Egyptian. 25 And he supposed that his brethren understood that God was granting them deliverance through him, but they did not understand"* (Acts 7:24–25).

6 The Hebrew word for "kill" (*harōg*) is used. This is a different verb than God's command in the Decalogue, "You shall not murder" (*retzakh*). In a court of law, Moses could not rightly be charged with premeditated murder; he went to check on the condition of his people, not kill a man. A jury would weigh evidence as to whether his action was justifiable homicide, but God is our ultimate judge.

Where is God?

God is not visible in this section of our story. We do see in Moses' action evidence of both the sense of justice and conscience our Creator has hardwired into humanity.

It's a reminder to us that our motivations are not hidden from the LORD. In the words of King David:

> *1 O LORD, You have searched me and known me.*
> *2 You know when I sit down and when I rise up;*
> *You understand my thought from afar.*
> *3 You scrutinize my path and my lying down,*
> *And are intimately acquainted with all my ways.*
> *4 Even before there is a word on my tongue,*
> *Behold, O LORD, You know it all.* (Psalm 139:1–4)

How different would our choices be if we remembered this reality?

Chapter 5

A Well and a Welcome

 Exodus 2:15–22

Moses has killed an Egyptian and buried the corpse. But the deed itself isn't covered up, so he has a choice to make which will change both his circumstances and his destiny.

Pharaoh learns of his daughter's adopted son's deed. In response, he determines to kill Moses, who in turn escapes to Midian[1] to find sanctuary. He finds himself at a well seeking water.

Already in the Bible's narrative we have seen how wells can provide the setting to romance stories. In Genesis 24, Abraham's servant prayed for a "divine appointment" with God's choice of a bride for Isaac. In answer, Rebekah appeared at the well in Nahor and draws water for the servant and his camels. Five chapters later, Jacob shows

---

1 Midian, the son of Abraham and Keturah (Genesis 25:1–2), settled in the northwestern Arabian desert. Moses made the long journey across the Sinai Peninsula to get far from Pharaoh's wrath.

up at a well in Haran and assists Rachel in watering Laban's flock.

So, when Moses in Midian encounters seven maidens, daughters of the local priest,[2] at the town well, diligent students of the Word pay attention. As Jacob had done, Moses assists the girls in drawing water for their flocks.

When local shepherds show up and chase the girls away, Moses stands up to them[3] and prevails. The girls return home and relate the story to their father[4] about the "Egyptian"[5] stranger who confronted the bullies. Dad wants to know why they didn't invite the hero home for dinner, which they then do.

The meal must have gone well because Moses not only sticks around but becomes a member of the family, marrying the daughter named Zipporah. Their union is blessed with a son, whom Moses names Gershom ("a stranger there"), reflecting his own status as a foreign resident in Midian. A lot of living is condensed in a few verses in our narrative.

---

2 This is the first mention of a "cohen" (priest) in Exodus. Genesis records Abraham's meeting with Melchizedek, *"a priest of God Most High"* (14:18). Joseph marries Asenath, *"the daughter of Potiphera priest of On"* (Genesis 41:45), whom we assume to be a follower of the Egyptian gods. We don't find out Jethro's theology until Exodus 18:11 when he testifies, *"Now I know that the LORD is greater than all the gods."*

3 This is the "reverse image" of the story in Genesis 24 where Abraham's servant meets Rebekah at the well in Nahor. She draws water for him and his camels. But in both cases a wedding results from a "chance encounter."

4 The father is named Reuel in Exodus 2:18 but in 3:1 and thereafter he is called Jethro. He is a Midianite (see footnote 1), not to be confused with the Reuel who was Esau's son.

5 Though Moses obviously has not forgotten his "Hebrew roots," he was identified by the girls as Egyptian – the culture that shaped the first four decades of his life.

Fear factor/Misery index:

Moses' lot in life has markedly changed. True, he no longer enjoys his status as a prince, but as a fugitive who has committed a capital offense, he's at least out of danger of being executed.

Moses' action to protect the girls against the Midianite shepherds demonstrates strength of character. He is now establishing a new life far from Pharaoh's grasp, with a wife and son for whom to care. But his improved lot is in stark contrast to his birth family's situation back in Egypt.

Where is God?

In Moses' life the LORD's hand is unseen to this point. But we do see in the circumstances of his life that Moses is protected from harm and provided with a family. The next 40 years will slide past without comment in our text. We have no insight into Moses' marriage, how he was as a dad, or the state of his spiritual health. Four decades of kicking sheep dung did nothing to enhance a prince's résumé. The pasture was a giant step-down from the palace.

So far as we know, Moses had no clue what lay in store for him. Did he grow weary in the daily grind of life? Did he share the sentiments another shepherd, David, would one day pen?

> *15 As for man, his days are like grass;*
> *As a flower of the field, so he flourishes.*

> *16 When the wind has passed over it, it is no more,*
> *And its place acknowledges it no longer*
> (Psalm 103:15–16).

We do have a clear clue Moses knows Midian is a foreign country when he names Gershom. But where is home? Egypt? Or is there yet an echo in his heart of Joseph's parting words generations prior? *"I am about to die, but God will surely take care of you and bring you up from this land to the land which He promised on oath to Abraham, to Isaac, and to Jacob"* (Genesis 50:24).

Chapter 6

Who Hears When We Cry?

Exodus 2:23–25

"Now it came about in the course of those many days that the king of Egypt died"[1] (2:23a). Good news for Moses, perhaps, but he's long miles away and unaffected by Pharaoh's death. Will the change in regime mean better treatment[2] for the suffering Hebrews?

Sadly, no. *"And the sons of Israel sighed because of the bondage, and they cried out ..."* (2:23b). What human being cannot relate to sighing and crying when life gets really tough? And remains rough over years?

---

1 When a king dies, old enmities usually die with him, and former fugitives may feel the liberty to return home. We see a New Testament parallel to this when Joseph, adoptive father of Yeshua (Jesus of Nazareth), returns to Israel with his family after Herod's death (Matthew 2:19–21).

2 As one example of hope for improved conditions with a new administration, when King Solomon died the citizens of Israel appealed to his son Rehoboam for tax relief. Rather than reducing taxes, the new king chose to listen to his younger advisers and increase the levies. The ensuing tax revolt split the kingdom in two. (See 1 Kings 12.)

The text continues:

> *... and their cry for help because of their bondage rose up to God. 24 So God heard their groaning; and God remembered His covenant with Abraham, Isaac, and Jacob. 25 God saw the sons of Israel, and God took notice of them.*

We note that while the text does not specifically state the Israelites cried out to the LORD,[3] their cry rose up to Him. Every year in the Passover Haggadah[4] we are reminded of this text. Emphasis is placed on the Almighty's actions: God heard, God remembered, God saw, and God took notice.

Fear factor/Misery index:

The Hebrews' longsuffering situation remains unchanged. "Sighing," "crying," and "groaning" define the very human response to intense and prolonged suffering. Daily life is miserable, and with the baby boys all being murdered, what hope is there for the future of Jewish people? How difficult must it have been to cling to the strong promises God made to Abraham, Isaac, and Jacob in those dark days, with no relief in sight.

---

3 On at least three occasions (8:12, 15:25, 17:4) Moses cries out "to the LORD," as do the Hebrews when pursued by Pharaoh's army at the Red Sea (14:10).

4 The Haggadah is the booklet used to retell the Exodus story each year. If you would like to experience a Messiah in the Passover Seder, please visit lifeinmessiah.org/host-a-passover-seder. You can also obtain a copy of LIFE's Haggadah at lifeinmessiah.org/seder-packet-resources.

Where is God?

Now, however, our narrator pulls back the veil of heaven to show us that God is attentive to His people's needs. He actively listens, sees, and pays attention. And indeed, He does remember His covenant with the patriarchs.

This is a great reminder to us that God's silence or seeming inaction does not indicate He is unaware or doesn't care. We easily grow impatient – like a child who daily digs up a newly planted seed, wondering why it doesn't sprout. It is good to be reminded of the character of our Creator revealed in such passages as this one in Psalm 34:

> *15 The eyes of the LORD are toward the righteous*
> *And His ears are open to their cry.*
> *16 The face of the LORD is against evildoers,*
> *To cut off the memory of them from the earth.*
> *17 The righteous cry, and the LORD hears*
> *And delivers them out of all their troubles.*
> *18 The LORD is near to the brokenhearted*
> *And saves those who are crushed in spirit.*

Chapter 7

A Dramatic Encounter with God

Decades have passed since Moses fled Egypt. We picture a sun-weathered man, now pushing 80,[1] tending his father-in-law's sheep in the western Arabian wilderness. On Mount Horeb[2] he has a personal encounter with divinity for the first time. And it is quite a story!

The saga begins with Moses' attention being drawn to a blazing bush that is not consumed by the flames. In the midst of the fire is *"the angel of the LORD."*[3] Then we are told, *"When the LORD saw that he turned aside*

---

1 Exodus 7:7 tells us Moses was 80 when he spoke with Pharaoh.

2 Here Horeb is called "the mountain of God." The same description is given to Mount Sinai in Exodus 24:13. The two names are used interchangeably in the Tanakh; see Deuteronomy 29:1, 1 Kings 8:9, and Psalm 106:19 as examples.

3 This is the first of 56 references to "the angel of the LORD" in the Tanakh. A study of these passages reveals a singular personage ("*the* angel" not "*an* angel") closely identified with God. For example, in Genesis 16:10–11 "the angel of the LORD" speaks to Hagar. In verse 13 Hagar indicates she "called the name of the LORD who spoke to her [the] 'God who sees.'"

to look, God called to him from the midst of the bush and said,[4] *'Moses, Moses!'"* (3:4).

Many religious systems have impersonal deities. Yet the God of the Bible not only is personal – He desires relationship. The Creator who knows both the number and names of the stars (Isaiah 40:26) also knows each of our names.[5] King David marvels in Psalm 8:

> *3 When I consider Your heavens, the work of Your fingers,*
> *The moon and the stars, which You have ordained;*
> *4 What is man that You take thought of him,*
> *And the son of man that You care for him?*

There is purpose to this "divine appointment." After warning Moses he is on holy ground, God introduces Himself – once again demonstrating how personally He relates to individuals. *"I am the God of your father, the God of Abraham, the God of Isaac, and the God of Jacob"* (3:6a).

He is in the process of becoming "the God of Moses" as well. Understanding dawns. Moses is not merely witnessing the unusual (an on-fire bush which doesn't turn to ash). He is in the presence of the Almighty. Fearful of looking at God (and who wouldn't be?), he hides his face (3:6b).[6]

---

4 This is not God's first appearance in fire; see Genesis 15:12–18. How God reveals Himself to mankind makes an interesting Bible study.

5 More than that, He knows even the number of hairs on our heads (Matthew 10:30)!

6 What a contrast to the Moses who later will ask God to reveal His glory to him (33:18).

Fear factor/Misery index

The fear mentioned in these verses is Moses' very appropriate response to finding himself in the presence of the Holy One of Israel. We may consider two aspects of fearing God. One is a powerful reverential awe which we see here as Moses hides his face.[7] Indeed, God will later affirm to Moses, *"You cannot see My face, for no man can see Me and live!"* (Exodus 33:20).

It is this "fear of the LORD" that the Psalms connect with so many benefits such as goodness and blessing.[8] Proverbs tells us *"the fear of the LORD is the beginning of wisdom"* (Proverbs 9:10) and connects fearing God with riches, honor, and life (Proverbs 22:4).

That's the good kind of fear! But a second fear of our holy God is the terror sinners experience when they face Him as judge. Scripture describes *"a terrifying expectation of judgment and the fury of a fire which will consume the adversaries ... 'The Lord will judge His people.' It is a terrifying thing to fall into the hands of the living God"* (Hebrews 10:27,30b–31).

Where is God?

That question is easy to answer in this passage. God has made a dramatic entrance into our story in a highly

---

7 Isaiah's response to his vision of the "high and lifted up" LORD was, *"Woe is me, for I am ruined! Because I am a man of unclean lips, and I live among a people of unclean lips; for my eyes have seen the King, the LORD of hosts"* (Isaiah 6:5).

8 Psalm 31:19; 112:1; 115:13; 128:1–4.

unusual way! And Moses is about to discover how radically his life will shift as a result.

Chapter 8
The God Who Comes to Deliver

Exodus 3:7–10

The LORD has more in mind than simply introducing Himself to Moses. He begins to reveal His purpose for this encounter by restating what we learned at the end of Exodus 2: *"I have surely seen the affliction of My people who are in Egypt, and have given heed to their cry because of their taskmasters, for I am aware of their sufferings"* (3:7).

Hearing this firsthand, in the LORD's very presence no less, answers the question, "Does God even know what's happening to me?" The doubled verb form in Hebrew, "seeing I have seen," intensifies the reality that yes, He truly is paying attention. He has heard their cry and is aware of the suffering of the enslaved Jewish people.

So God knows. But does He care?

"So I have come down[1] to deliver them from the power of the Egyptians, and to bring them up from that land to a good and spacious land, to a land flowing with milk and honey ..." (3:8).

This at last is what suffering hearts cry out for – deliverance from on high! Relief is coming! And God Himself is going to intervene on their behalf.

But the LORD is promising more than escape from bondage. He is going to bring the children of Israel to the land[2] He covenanted to give to Abraham and his descendants![3]

Fear factor/Misery index

The Hebrews back in Egypt still live in a nightmare that seemingly has no end. Deliverance is coming, but we have no record that anyone is aware of this.

---

1 The idea that God Himself has come down to deliver is reflected in the Passover Haggadah: "The LORD brought us out of Egypt not by an angel, not by a seraph, not by a messenger, but by the Holy One Himself, blessed is He."

2 In Exodus 3:10 God refers to the Hebrews as *"My people, the sons of Israel."* This is the first of 130 times *ami* (My people) is found in the Tanakh. In every case but one (Isaiah 19:25, where Egypt is in view in the prophetic future), it refers to the Jewish people.

3 In case we have forgotten where the Promised Land is, God lists six people groups who inhabited the territory at that time. When compared to the longer list of 10 peoples inhabiting the Land (Genesis 15:19–21), the Kenites, Kenizzites, Kadmonites, Rephaim, and Girgashites are missing, but in Exodus 3:8 the Hivites are added. This may reflect population shifts since Abraham's day – or just a shortened list.

Where is God?

God not only shows up, but communicates clearly to Moses, assuring him help is on the way. But at this juncture only Moses in Midian is aware the LORD has seen the sufferings of the children of Israel and heard their cries.

But where was God when a wicked pharaoh arose to afflict the Hebrews? (And by extension, where was He when the six million died in the Holocaust? Or when terrorists torment, kidnap, and slaughter women, children, and grandparents? Or when a novel coronavirus strikes globally?)

Of course, those who believe in a sovereign, omniscient God would affirm He was well aware of the dire circumstances of Abraham's offspring before He appeared to Moses. He just hadn't told Moses about His plan yet.

Or had He?

When the LORD "cut"[4] the covenant with Abraham back in Genesis 15, He spelled out in some detail what yet lay in store for future generations:

> *13 God said to Abram, "Know for certain that your descendants will be strangers in a land that is not theirs, where they will be enslaved and oppressed four hundred years. 14 But I will also judge the nation whom they will serve,*

---

4 In Hebrew, the word used for "made" in Genesis 15:18 (*On that day the LORD made a covenant with Abram*) is כָּרַת, literally "to cut."

and afterward they will come out with many possessions. 15 As for you, you shall go to your fathers in peace; you will be buried in a good old age. 16 Then in the fourth generation they will return here, for the iniquity of the Amorites is not yet complete."

What may we learn from this? Our suffering may seem both endless and purposeless. We often don't have an answer to our "Why, God?"

But the passage from Genesis 15, which is quoted every year in the reading of the Passover Haggadah in Jewish homes around the world, should hearten every believer in the God of Abraham. We have a "know-for-certain God" who has a purpose for His people. And His purposes are always good – even when our circumstances are not.

Chapter 9
"Who Am I?"

In our story, Moses has been listening to the voice of God speaking from a flaming bush. We may readily believe Moses is heartened to hear of the LORD's concern for the children of Israel – Moses' own relatives who continue to suffer hardship as slaves in Egypt. Moreover, God has declared, **"I have come down to deliver them"** *(3:7–8).*

Great news! Who doesn't desire divine intervention for our benefit?

But what's this Moses hears? *"Therefore, come now, and I will send you to Pharaoh, so that you may bring My people, the sons of Israel, out of Egypt"* (3:10).

For 40 years Moses has been tending his father-in-law's flocks and raising his own family. How often might his mind have drifted back to Egypt, remembering his years growing up in the palace? Wondering how his family is holding up under oppression? Wishing something could be done to help them? He had tried to help. But that effort to defend a fellow Hebrew who was being beaten cost Moses everything.

And now God is telling me to go back? Back to Egypt? Back to Pharaoh who tried to kill me!? And to what end? To deliver Israel out of Egypt? How am I to do that?

The text doesn't tell us if Moses' thoughts were anything like this, but it does record his response: ***"Who am I, that I should go to Pharaoh, and that I should bring the sons of Israel out of Egypt?"*** (3:11).

Moses has not been training to lead a special forces team on a hostage rescue operation. He doesn't command an army prepared to take on Egypt's powerful military. He's an 80-year-old sheepherder. Whatever his education back in his palace years may have prepared him for, he knows he's not qualified for this job. Who better than Moses would understand how daunting it would be to stand before Pharaoh and demand the release of his workforce?

"Who am I?" is not in itself a bad question. "Know thyself" is good counsel. An honest assessment of our capabilities is wise when considering options.

But it's different when God is giving out assignments. Who better than He knows our qualifications – or lack thereof? We see in Scripture that the Sovereign of the Universe often chooses unlikely means and flawed people to carry out His purposes.[1] "Little is much when God is in it"; He gets the greater glory when tremendous obstacles are overcome and hardships are endured by His strengthening hand.

Moses then hears, *"Certainly I will be with you"*[2] (3:12a).

If we ever wondered what it looks like to step out in obedience by faith, the LORD's next words provide a shining example. *"And this shall be the sign to you that it is I who have sent you: when you have brought the people out of Egypt, you shall worship God at this mountain"* (3:12b).

What kind of assurance is this? In essence, Moses will have proof his assignment truly was from the Almighty only after he has carried out God's instruction! What a great example of *"we walk by faith, not by sight"* (2 Corinthians 5:7)!

But Moses apparently is thinking through the "what would it look like if ..." scenario.

> *Then Moses said to God, "Behold, I am going to the sons of Israel, and I will say to them, 'The God of your fathers has sent me to you.' Now they*

---

1 What are the implications of this for you and me? If our default answer to God's call is, "Who am I?" then how long does it take to change our response to "Here am I. Send me!"? See Isaiah 6:1–8 for another example.

2 God reassures many of His people with these comforting words; e.g., Isaac (Genesis 26:3), Jacob (Genesis 31:3), Joshua (Deuteronomy 31:23; Joshua 1:5; 3:7), Gideon (Judges 6:16), Jeroboam (1 Kings 11:38), and the nation of Israel (Isaiah 43:2). Yeshua also promised His followers, "I am with you always, even to the end of the age" (Matthew 28:20).

may say to me, 'What is His name?' What shall I say to them?" (3:13).

"Who am I?" may be an important introspective question for contemplation. But "Who are You?" is a critically vital inquiry when seeking to know the Author of life and finding ultimate meaning for our existence.

We note again the danger of assigning motives to Moses' speech or action. Is he already committed to obeying this voice from the burning bush? Is he stalling for time while he considers obstacles he'll likely encounter? Or does he genuinely just need to know with Whom he is talking, given what's at stake?[3]

God said to Moses, "I AM WHO I AM";[4] and He said, "Thus you shall say to the sons of Israel, 'I AM has sent me to you'" (3:14).

---

3 We could wish we had more details on exactly when Moses becomes the man of faith who is praised in Hebrews 11:23–29. How well-acquainted with the "God of his fathers" was Moses? We can only speculate on how much his parents were able to teach him before handing him over to Pharaoh's daughter. It is highly doubtful that the God of the Hebrews would have been given much attention by whomever may have instructed Moses on religion in the palace. We have no record of interaction between Moses and the Hebrews before he slew the Egyptian. And Jethro was a pagan priest. Is Moses wanting more than God's "business card" here when asking His identity?

4 The Hebrew verb God used in verse 12, "*I will be with you*" is the same form found duplicated in verse 14. "*I will be* Who *I will be*" is a statement of the Uncreated Creator's self-existence.

Further, God now[5] reveals His "personal Name"[6] to Moses. *"Thus you shall say to the sons of Israel, 'The LORD, the God of your fathers, the God of Abraham, the God of Isaac, and the God of Jacob,[7] has sent me to you.' This is My name forever, and this is My memorial-name to all generations"* (3:15).

Fear factor/Misery index

The wonder of this divine appearance which initially struck Moses with fear has abated to the point that Moses is able to converse with the Almighty. But the daunting task to which he is being called is surely a matter with which Moses wrestles.

Where is God?

God is not only personally present with Moses, He is promising to go with him on assignment to Egypt. What

---

5 This "nominal form" of the verb "to be" ("I am") is not found in Exodus until Chapter 3. Exodus 3:2 introduces "the angel of the LORD"; in verse 4 "the LORD saw." "LORD" appears 340 times in Exodus, of which 16 use the combined form "LORD GOD."

6 When reading sacred texts aloud, Jewish people replace this special "ineffable" (not-to-be-pronounced) Name with "Adonai" or "HaShem" (literally, "the Name") as a way of preserving its holiness – in keeping with the commandment not to take the LORD's name in vain (20:7). The same conviction is why names of deity such as God or LORD are not spelled out. "J-hovah" was not introduced as a possible pronunciation until 1520 but not likely correct. (See "H3068 - Yᵊhōvâ - Strong's Hebrew Lexicon [NASB 95]," Blue Letter Bible, blueletterbible.org/lexicon/h3068/nasb95/wlc/0-1/.)

7 This is an echo of how God introduced Himself to Moses in verse 6, with the addition of His four-consonant personal name. Interestingly, "the God of your fathers" is plural here; in verse 6 it is "father," perhaps an indication that Amram (Moses' father), of whom we are told little, was a follower of the God of Abraham.

a heartening prospect – and a reality Moses will come to rely upon as this adventure continues!

"I will never leave you or forsake you" is one of Scripture's most precious promises. His enduring presence is the pledge of God to the nation of Israel[8] and to individuals like Jacob and Joshua.[9]

Before He departed for heaven, the Lord Jesus promised His disciples, "I am with you always; even to the end of the age" (Matthew 28:20). Whatever our circumstances, believers can count on Messiah walking alongside us until He returns for us (John 14:1–3).

---

8 Deuteronomy 31:6, 8; Isaiah 41:10.

9 Genesis 28:15; Joshua 1:9.

Chapter 10
The Divine Strategy Revealed

The Almighty has introduced Himself to Moses as the God of his fathers, with the intention of sending him to deliver the Hebrews from Egypt. But how will this be accomplished?

Moses now receives his "marching instructions" from the LORD, who begins, ***"Go and gather the elders[1] of Israel together"*** (3:16a). Doubtless Moses' initial audience will be the influencers and decision makers of the enslaved Hebrews.

Included with these orders is the script of the message God wishes Moses to communicate. He begins with the now-familiar formula, ***"the God of your fathers"*** (3:16c), whom He names individually once more.

---

1 This is the first reference in Scripture to this esteemed group; they are mentioned 11 times in Exodus and will play an important role in Israel henceforth.

Why is it necessary to repeat the patriarchs' names? We may surmise all kinds of reasons. Certainly, in the sea of pagan deities worshiped in Egypt, the LORD wants to be known to the Hebrew people as the One who made Himself known to their forebears. He is the One who "cut the covenant" with Abraham (Genesis 15) and repeated His promises to Isaac and Jacob. Perhaps invoking their names will stir up the elders' memories of stories of those events carried throughout their generations.

"I am indeed concerned about you and what has been done to you in Egypt" (3:16d) would be reassuring to a people who must have wondered, *Where is God amidst our suffering?*

The next verse records the promise, *"I will bring you up out of the afflictions of Egypt"* (deliverance!) to the Promised Land (restoration!).

The LORD also informs Moses that the elders will respond positively and accompany him to the king of Egypt. Together they are to announce that "the God of the Hebrews" has met with them. The initial request will only be for a three-day release from their labors so the Hebrews can *"sacrifice to the LORD our God"* (3:18).

> *19 But I know that the King of Egypt will not permit you to go, except under compulsion. 20 So I will stretch out My hand and strike Egypt with all My miracles which I shall do in the midst of it; and after that he will let you go.*

"But I know" from God's mouth to Moses' ears should serve as a reminder of His omniscience. "After that he will let you go" provides assurance that God's "game plan" has a known (and positive) outcome. This is a wonderful "theology sandwich" – with miracles in the middle!

But wait – there's more!

"I will grant this people favor in the sight of the Egyptians" (3:21) indicates that God will also work in the hearts of the Egyptian people. Yes, our Sovereign LORD purposes to bless His people even through those who have oppressed them.[2] The women of Egypt will supply the Hebrews with "articles of silver and articles of gold, and clothing"[3] (3:23).

Fear factor/Misery index

The "afflictions of Egypt" are once again referenced. How much blood, sweat, and tears have been shed over these years of generational bondage only God knows.

Where is God?

But God DOES know. He remembers His covenants from the past. He is aware of the sufferings of His people in the present. King David will later write, *"You have taken account of my wanderings; put my tears in Your bottle. Are they not in Your book?"* (Psalm 56:8).

2 To glimpse how limitless is God's grace, see His wonderful yet-to-be-fulfilled promise of blessing to Egypt in Isaiah 19:24–25.

3 The Hebrews will receive "back pay" in abundance for their forced servitude, as God had promised Abraham in Genesis 15:13–14.

And God knows His plans for our future. Omniscience, knowing the end from the beginning, is one of His attributes which sets Him apart from all creatures.

In addition to His foreknowledge, He is in control of the future. As Isaiah states, *"Declaring the end from the beginning, and from ancient times things which have not been done, saying, 'My purpose will be established, and I will accomplish all My good pleasure'"* (Isaiah 46:10).

We are reminded from this passage that included in God's perfect plan book for His people are difficult pages, which sometimes extend into chapters. If we only focus on our circumstances, especially when suffering is prolonged, we will despair.

The remedy? This beautiful Psalm of Ascents speaks to our hearts in fearful times, when our enemy seeks to convince us that God has gone to sleep.

> *1 I will lift up my eyes to the mountains;*
> *From where shall my help come?*
> *2 My help comes from the LORD,*
> *Who made heaven and earth.*
> *3 He will not allow your foot to slip;*
> *He who keeps you will not slumber.*
> *4 Behold, He who keeps Israel*
> *Will neither slumber nor sleep.*
> *5 The Lord is your keeper;*
> *The Lord is your shade on your right hand.*
> *6 The sun will not smite you by day,*
> *Nor the moon by night.*

7 The Lord will protect you from all evil;
He will keep your soul.
8 The Lord will guard your going out and your
coming in
From this time forth and forever (Psalm 121:1–8).

Note well: This Psalm is all about who God is and what He will do on our behalf. The only "I will" for us is to "lift up our eyes" in faith to the Eternal Source of our protection.

Chapter 11

What's My Excuse?

Moses' initial response to God's "I will send you to Pharaoh" was "Who am I?" The LORD has revealed Himself in a very personal way, promising to be with Moses in this daunting venture. Moses has God's assurance that, though victory won't be swift or easy, ultimate success is assured.

Having received such divine assurance, Moses should be "good to go," right?

Not quite. He continues asking the "but what if" questions as he considers his options.

"What if they will not believe me or listen to what I say? For they may say, 'The LORD has not appeared to you'" (4:1).

Before criticizing Moses unduly, we would do well to put ourselves in his sandals (though at this time he's standing barefoot – next to a flaming bush in which the angel of the LORD has appeared). God has done most of the talking, but unless He is speaking exceedingly slowly or with long pauses, the entire conversation to this point is less than four minutes long.

One may imagine that Moses is singularly transfixed by the scene before him. What in his 80 years of life thus far would compare to a divine appearance in an on-fire-but-unconsumed shrub?

The release of his people from bondage would be a joyful prospect, doubtless. But that he himself would return to Egypt to effect their escape likely was beyond anything Moses had fantasized. Idealistic dreams of heroic glory are the stuff of youth. Eight decades of living – four of them guarding flocks in a desert – would tend to erode visions of daring exploits.

Perhaps Moses is thinking, *Even if I DID go, who would ever listen to such a fantastic tale? I'm having a hard time believing this is happening myself. How would I ever convince others?*

Thankfully, God understands Moses is struggling to take in this mind-blowing experience.

"What's that in your hand?" (4:2).

God doesn't ask questions because He doesn't know the answers. He is not unfamiliar with a shepherd's staff.

He's teaching Moses by taking what is very familiar – a walking stick with a hook for rescuing a sheep from a ditch – to do something extraordinary.

When Moses obeys the LORD and throws down the staff, it transforms into a serpent from which Moses flees![1] At God's command, he grabs the serpent's tail and it returns to be his trusty walking stick.

Next comes "Object Lesson 2." Moses removes the hand God told him to place on his chest underneath his outer garment and finds it "leprous like snow" (v. 6). Before the horror of that disease has time to fully register, God has him repeat the process – and the hand is back to normal.

And if these two signs will not prove sufficient for the elders of Israel to believe Moses is indeed on a mission from God, a third sign will be provided: Nile water will be turned to blood.

One may imagine how Moses' head must be spinning. Obviously, he is experiencing the supernatural take place before his very eyes. But the assignment he's being given still is beyond Moses' perceived abilities.

"Please, Lord,[2] I have never been eloquent, neither recently nor in time past, nor since You have spoken

---

1 Thankfully "The Book of Moses" (the Torah/Pentateuch) records the frailties and foibles of our heroes, Moses included, as well as their exploits. They were like us! In contrast to another shepherd who in his youth killed a lion and a bear (1 Samuel 17:34–36), Moses "hightails it" at the sight of a serpent – though surely he had previously encountered many in his years in the desert.

2 Here Moses addresses God as "Adonai," not with His personal name, YHVH.

to Your servant; for I am slow of speech and slow of tongue" (4:10).

Don't you love the honesty in reporting here? *Um, Lord, I'm really not qualified for this spokesman job. You know, I've never been much of a speaker in the past, distant or recent. And actually, since we've been chatting you've restored my staff and healed my hand — but my tongue still doesn't work well.*

The LORD responds with two rhetorical questions: Who creates mouths? And who makes people able to speak or see? And He answers with a third, *"Is it not I, the LORD?"* (4:11).

God has already promised to be with Moses (3:12). Now He promises, *"I, even I [the One who created you just as you are], will be with your mouth, and teach you what you are to say"* (4:12).

But Moses REALLY doesn't want to take on this task! *"Please, Lord, now send the message by whomever You will [just so it isn't ME!]"* (4:13).

For the first time in the biblical record, the LORD is angry (4:14).[3] But He extends grace, informing Moses that his eloquent brother Aaron is on his way to help with communications:

---

3 When Abraham bargained with God to spare Sodom, he twice entreated Him not to be angry (Genesis 18:30, 32), but there is no incident of God being angry until Exodus 4. (We do see other prior expression of divine emotions, e.g., in Genesis 6:6 where He was sorry He had made man and was grieved in His heart.)

15 You are to speak to [Aaron] and put the words in his mouth; and I, even I, will be with your mouth and his mouth, and I will teach you what you are to do. 16 Moreover, he shall speak for you to the people; and he will be as a mouth for you and you will be as God to him.

With a final, "Oh, and don't forget your staff – you'll need it," this singular divine encounter ends.

Fear factor/Misery index

Moses' misery is centered on his assessment of his own lack of ability. Even after the LORD demonstrates supernatural signs (having a conversation with God in a burning bush is not sufficient), the 80-year-old Moses is not on board. A return trip to Egypt would have its own perils. Demanding Pharaoh release his slaves? That's a job for someone else!

Where is God?

We see the LORD's patience demonstrated as He deals with a reluctant prophet. He promises to be present; He demonstrates His power. He reminds Moses of His sovereignty in creation. And yes, He gets angry.

"In wrath remember mercy" (Habakkuk 3:2) is exactly what we see on display here. God neither destroys nor dismisses Moses. Instead, He provides the extra assistance Moses needs to accept the assignment he's been given.

As the psalmist says, *"[God] Himself knows our frame; He is mindful that we are but dust"* (Psalm 103:14).

Chapter 12
The Adventure Begins

Having God's assurance of His presence and Aaron's assistance, Moses is now willing to obey the LORD – despite His admonition that it wouldn't be easy. True enough! Even the early stages of this expedition to free his people will be challenging.

Moses' first stop after the burning bush is to see his father-in-law. Apparently, Moses doesn't relate to Jethro the details of his encounter with the Almighty. He simply asks for a "leave of absence" to do a "wellness check" on his relatives. Jethro consents (4:18).

The LORD continues to speak to Moses,[1] first assuring him that those in Egypt who sought to kill him have

---

1 Exodus 4:19. In most instances, the Torah does not specify the fashion in which God spoke to Moses after the encounter with the angel of the LORD at the burning bush. Exodus 33:11 does tell us, "Thus the LORD used to speak to Moses face to

died.[2] Moses sets out from Midian; his wife Zipporah and their boys ride along on a donkey. No mention is made of what baggage or provisions were packed for the journey across the Sinai Peninsula. But, in obedience to God's instruction, Moses had "the staff of God" in his hand (4:20).

The LORD continues to prepare Moses for what lies ahead. Back at the burning bush God had informed Moses that He knew *"the king of Egypt will not let you go, except under compulsion"* (3:19). Now He gives insight into the Egyptian king's obstinance after he has seen all the powerful signs Moses will perform. God *"will harden [Pharaoh's] heart so that he will not let the people go"* (4:21).

In musical terms, God is giving Moses the overture to the symphony that will follow. In literary terms, He is introducing the cast of characters and providing glimpses of the plot. We do well to pay attention here!

> *22 Then you shall say to Pharaoh, "Thus says the LORD, 'Israel is My son, My firstborn. 23 So I said to you, "Let My son go that he may serve Me"; but you have refused to let him go. Behold, I will kill your son, your firstborn.'"*

In the strategic conflict which is about to unfold, Pharaoh remains the nemesis. Of course, the LORD is the hero of this piece (and of every other story!). Moses and Aaron

---

face, just as a man speaks to his friend." Numbers 12:8 and Deuteronomy 34:10 also describe their unique relationship.

2 Moses need not wonder if the "statute of limitations" was in effect; after 40 years, his assassins had expired!

are His agents. God has already identified Israel, the victims of Egypt's abuse, as "My people" (3:7).

But the stakes are demonstrably heightened when God identifies Israel as *"My son, My firstborn son"*[3] (4:22). His instruction to Pharaoh is, *"Let My son go that he may serve Me"*[4] (4:23). The time has come to liberate the Creator's firstborn from being Pharaoh's slaves so they may freely serve the LORD![5]

A further jarring episode follows in our narrative. Moses is journeying with his family toward Egypt in obedience to God's direction. During an overnight stop, *"the LORD met [Moses] and sought to put him to death"* (4:24). God only relents after Zipporah circumcises one of their sons[6] (4:25–26).

The scene shifts again as Aaron, following God's instruction, journeys to meet Moses at *"the mountain of God"* (4:27). After what must have been a very joyful reunion, Moses provides his brother with the details of his encounter with the LORD and the words that Aaron is to pronounce as the drama unfolds (4:28).

---

3 In many cultures the firstborn son holds a privileged position in the family, including leadership and the greater portion of inheritance attached to the birthright. "My firstborn son" emphasizes the value God places on the Jewish people.

4 The Hebrew word avod may be translated "serve" or "worship."

5 As we will see, the consequence for not obeying God will cost Pharaoh the life of his own firstborn son – at the Almighty's own hand.

6 Given the fact that God desists from killing Moses after his son is circumcised, we may infer the failure to enact the covenantal sign of circumcision (Genesis 17:10) was at issue. Zipporah's strong reaction leads some to think she may have objected to the procedure (which perhaps had been performed on her firstborn, as only one circumcision is recorded here) – but where the text is silent only conjecture remains.

Without further fanfare, we are told the brothers, safely arrived in Egypt, assemble the elders of Israel. Aaron relates God's message and the validating signs are performed in the eyes of the Hebrews (4:29–30).

"So the people believed; and when they heard that the Lord was concerned about the sons of Israel and that He had seen their affliction, then they bowed low and worshiped" (4:31). What a wonderful response by the longsuffering Jewish people as they were powerfully reminded of God's sovereign care for them.

Fear factor/Misery index

What is it like when God reveals Himself as an adversary? Pharaoh has yet to feel the weight of that reality, but Moses had a moment when his very life was in danger of being snuffed out by the Almighty. "The fear of the LORD" includes terror when He judges. Asaph writes, *"You, even You, are to be feared; and who may stand in Your presence when once You are angry?"* (Psalm 76:7).

"The fear of the LORD" also includes reverential awe. We see this displayed by the Israelites who respond in worship when learning of God's tender care for them.

Where is God?

God's actions are seen throughout this section: He instructs Moses (and seeks his life!). He directs Aaron and empowers him to perform signs. God's heart is also seen as He speaks for the first time of the nation of Israel as His firstborn son.[7]

The actors now are all in place. The stage is set for one of the greatest showdowns in all of history!

7 See Deuteronomy 14:1 and Jeremiah 31:20 for echoes of this Father-son relationship.

Chapter 13

When the Going Gets Harder

 Exodus 5:1–21

Success! Moses and Aaron have performed the signs to authenticate the message of the God of Israel to His people. The children of Israel believed! They bowed and worshiped the God of their fathers. But a tougher audience awaits.

The next stop for Moses and Aaron: Pharaoh's office. We don't have details about how long they waited for an audience with the king of Egypt or if they gave a reason for seeking an appointment.

Think of this. Moses and Aaron are representing a foreign deity (and one identified with a subjugated people, at that). In His name they will demand Pharaoh's labor force be granted a religious holiday. In starkest terms they make their pronouncement to a powerful ruler: ***"Thus says the LORD, the God of Israel, 'Let My*** *people go that they may celebrate a feast to Me in the wilderness'"* (5:1).

"I do not know the LORD"

The warm reception the Jewish people had given to this message from the LORD is not mirrored in the palace. Pharaoh's scornful response: *"Who is the LORD that I should obey His voice to let Israel go? I do not know the LORD, and besides, I will not let Israel go"*[1] (5:2).

A command from the God of the Hebrews hasn't worked. Moses and Aaron explain further, this time in the form of a request. *"Please let us go ..."* (5:3).

They reason with the king that it's only a trip of three days into the desert for a worship service. (They'll be back within a week; what would that hurt?) And, after all, they don't want to make God angry – or pestilence and sword may result.

But Pharaoh's not buying it. *"Get back to work!"* (5:4).

As did his predecessor 80 years prior, this Egyptian potentate has taken note of how large the Hebrew population is. Losing even a day's work from this labor force is not something he's likely to consider (5:5).

---

1 At this point, had we been granted a quick scene change to the halls of heaven, we might hear God saying with a smile, "It's true, Pharaoh; you don't know Me. But you will ...!"

From bad to worse

The lives of the slaves already had been bitter enough to cause sighing, crying, and groaning (2:24–25). Conditions were about to get much worse.

Was it the insult of being ordered around by the God of a slave people that set off Egypt's king? Pharaoh calls together his taskmasters and the Hebrew foremen they had appointed to supervise the work. The decree is handed down that henceforth the Hebrews need to gather the straw to make the bricks used for construction. Oh, and no drop in the production output will be tolerated (5:6–9).

Word gets passed down to the Jewish people, who now spread out over Egypt in search of straw. The taskmasters bear down on them, berating them for failing to meet the fixed production quotas (5:10–14).

No rescue in sight

The Hebrew foremen plead their case before Pharaoh, who will hear none of it. *"You are lazy, very lazy; therefore you say, 'Let us go and sacrifice to the LORD'"* (5:15–18).

No lessening of pressure, no relief in sight. The foremen know they are in deep difficulty. And they are being blamed for the request for time off for a religious observance (5:19).

What comes next is a very human response to hardship: pushback against leadership. The foremen's appeals to Pharaoh were futile. Now Moses and Aaron are the targets of their anger. *"May the LORD look upon you and judge you, for you have made us odious in Pharaoh's sight and in the sight of his servants, to put a sword in their hand to kill us"* (5:20–21).

Fear factor/Misery index

Exodus 4 ended with the Hebrews holding a praise and worship service to the LORD, with the expectation of a quick delivery from what has been generations of bondage. We end this portion of Scripture with the Jewish people enduring even greater misery than before Moses and Aaron showed up to declare God's love and purpose. *"Hope deferred makes the heart sick"* (Proverbs 13:12).

Where is God?

Pharaoh's response to Moses and Aaron's "Thus says the LORD" is a snorted, *"Who is the LORD that I should obey His voice?"* (5:2a).

Lightning doesn't flash in the sky. The earth doesn't open up and swallow Pharaoh. But take note: The king's sneering dismissal of the God of Israel will not go unanswered.

A number of conversations are recorded in Exodus 5 – but God is silent here. He has already stated to Moses[2] that the road ahead will be rough.[3]

For the LORD, everything is on schedule. The assumptions, desires, and expectations of the children of Israel don't align with the divine timetable. Suffering humanity wants deliverance yesterday!

We measure life with a stopwatch; God uses a calendar to mark time. *"For a thousand years in Your sight are like yesterday when it passes by, or as a watch in the night"* (Psalm 90:4).

---

2 Exodus 3:19; 4:21.

3 And God had told Abraham that his descendants would be oppressed in a land not their own for 400 years (Genesis 15:13).

Chapter 14
When God Says "I Will"

Exodus 5:22–6:13

Moses and Aaron are in a tough spot. The only thing working right now is the Jewish people – and they are working overtime to try to keep up with the increased demands Pharaoh has placed upon them. The king won't listen, the taskmasters won't relent, and the Hebrew foremen are angry with the brothers who came promising deliverance. To whom can they turn?

"Then Moses returned to the LORD ..." (5:22a). Great idea! Amidst his frustrations he pours out his heart.

> *"O Lord, why have You brought harm to this people? Why did You ever send me? 23 Ever since I came to Pharaoh to speak in Your name, he has done harm to this people, and You have not delivered Your people at all."*

Laying blame at God's feet is a very human response to life's difficulties. Ever since Adam's *"the woman You gave me"* [so it's Your fault!] charge in Eden (Genesis 3:12), mankind has been prone to make the Sovereign of the Universe responsible for what has gone wrong. Disappointment provides very fertile ground for the enemy of our souls to sow seeds of discontent with the Almighty.

Moses makes his case: I did what You asked and represented You to Pharaoh. Not only did he not release the people, but he is making their lives far worse! Why in the world did you ever give me this mission in the first place?

The divine response

The LORD neither dismisses Moses nor rebukes him. He simply indicates the story is far from over. *"Now you will see what I shall do to Pharaoh; for under compulsion he will let them go"* (6:1).

That the God of Israel desires a personal relationship with His children is demonstrated by what He next tells Moses by way of reminder:

1. I am the LORD. (Exodus 6:2 echoes 3:14.)

2. I appeared to the patriarchs; they knew Me as God Almighty,[1] and I covenanted to give Canaan to them. (Exodus 6:3–4 echoes 3:15.)

---

1 "El Shaddai" appears five times in Genesis (17:1 is the first); "Shaddai" is also used alone to refer to the Almighty in 49:25. "The LORD" appears 165 times in Genesis beginning with the creation story in 2:4. Genesis 13:14 specifically says that Abram "called on the name of the LORD." Some infer from this that for the patriarchs the emphasis had been on God's powerful protection of individuals and

3. I am well aware of the sufferings of My people and I haven't forgotten my covenant with them. (Exodus 6:5 echoes 3:7; see also 2:24.)

The "I will" statements which follow, bracketed front and back by "I am the LORD," are God's declaration to the Israelites of His plan of action and purpose for His people:

1. *"I will bring you out from under the burdens of the Egyptians, and I will deliver you from their bondage" (6:6ab).*

2. *"I will also redeem you with an outstretched arm and with great judgments." (6:6c).*

3. *"Then I will take you for My people, and I will be your God" (6:7ab).*

4. *"I will bring you to the land which I swore to give to Abraham, Isaac, and Jacob, and I will give it to you for a possession" (6:8).*

"And you shall know"

Tucked into God's third "I will" is this statement: *"and you shall know that I am the LORD your God, who brought you out from under the burdens of the Egyptians"* (6:7c). God first declares His intention to adopt the Jewish people as His own after He delivers them. He then states, *"You shall know that I am the LORD your God."*

---

provision (of the Land in particular). Beginning in Exodus He relates to the nation as the great "I AM" who will redeem His people. "The LORD" is His "memorial-name" for all generations (3:15).

"Why, God?" is a question which often goes unanswered. Why did God intend Abraham's descendants to be in bondage in Egypt? Why have there been generations of suffering?

Here we are given insight into God's "why." One of His primary purposes in staging what is about to unfold is that His people truly would know the LORD.[2] Know Him as THEIR God. Know Him as THEIR Redeemer. Henceforth, He will remind them of this in two specific ways. He will institute Passover as the first holiday to be commemorated (12:17). And He will continue to refer to Himself as *"the LORD your God who brought you out of Egypt."*[3]

Armed with these specific assurances from the mouth of the Almighty, Moses returns to the Israelites to share the heartening message. *"But they did not listen to Moses on account of their despondency and cruel bondage"* (6:9b).

Fear factor/Misery index

Moses is miserable. Very miserable. Disappointment and discouragement fuel many fires of anger. But he stays on mission.

---

2 God says to Israel "that you may know that I am the LORD" four more times in Exodus: 10:2, 16:12, 29:46 and 31:13. Moses also tells them, "You will know that the LORD has brought you out of the land of Egypt" (16:6).

3 Indeed, this is how God begins the giving of the Ten Commandments on Mount Sinai (20:2). See also Exodus 29:46; Leviticus 11:45; 19:36; 22:33, 43; 25:38, 55; 26:13, 45; Numbers 15:41; Deuteronomy 5:6; Psalm 81:10. Many other times in the Tanakh God references bringing Israel out of bondage/Egypt in speaking to His people. And Moses (e.g., Exodus 16:6) and other prophets in Israel will also refer to the LORD as the One who performed this seminal event in Jewish history.

The children of Israel are miserable. And fed up. And losing hope. So much so that when Moses brings more words from the LORD, they don't want to hear it. When our eyes are downcast, focused on our troubles, traumas, and tragedies, it's easy for our ears to be closed to the promises of God's Word. And to allow our circumstances to determine our view of our Creator.

Satan delights to offer other options when our faith in the LORD shrinks. If God isn't coming through, then surely there is another way to ease the pain, find a detour, or seek satisfaction in something else.

The prophet Ezekiel provides details we don't find in Exodus (e.g., Ezekiel 20:5–9). Apparently, many of the Hebrews had begun to follow the idols of Egypt during the time of their captivity.[4]

Where is God?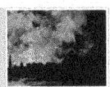

Thankfully, God is gracious, patient, and merciful. *"He has not dealt with us according to our sins, nor rewarded us according to our iniquities"* (Psalm 103:10).

> *The LORD will accomplish what concerns me;*
> *Your lovingkindness, O LORD, is everlasting;*

---

4 Piecing together the response of the Israelites in Exodus 4:29–31 (where they joyfully accepted the news of their pending redemption and worshiped the LORD) it would seem they initially agreed to God's precondition to forsake "the detestable things of their eyes." But, as Ezekiel 20:8 indicates, they decided to hang onto their Egyptian deities – likely when their lives grew more bitter after Moses went to Pharaoh to demand the release of the captives. How easy it is for faith to falter when adversity recurs!

> *Do not forsake the works of Your hands*
> (Psalm 138:8).

Nothing will thwart His eternal plan!

Chapter 15

"A Brother is Born for Adversity"

Exodus 6:14–7:7

Have you noticed God is never in a hurry? Three years before Moses was born, the LORD gave a son to Amram and Jochebed. Who would have foreseen the role Aaron would play in Israel's history 83 years later?

A key family tree

Biblical genealogies are vital records, as attested by the attention they are given. In Exodus 6:14–16a we have a repeat of Genesis 46:8–11. But where the Genesis record goes on to list the other sons and grandsons of Jacob/ Israel,[1] here in Exodus the focus narrows to the Levites. Of special note is the Levi → Kohath → Amram → Aaron and Moses lineage (6:16–20).

---

1 God changes Jacob's name to Israel in Genesis 32:28.

Aaron married Elisheva who bore him four sons: Nadab, Abihu, Eleazar and Ithamar (6:23). Eleazar's wife Putiel and son Phineas also are mentioned[2] (6:25).

Once more, for emphasis

Our author's purpose here in detailing the bloodline is to highlight the immediate role of two brothers:

> *26 It was the same Aaron and Moses to whom the LORD said, "Bring out the sons of Israel from the land of Egypt according to their hosts." 27 They were the ones who spoke to Pharaoh king of Egypt about bringing out the sons of Israel from Egypt; it was the same Moses and Aaron.*

Now the protagonists' identities are confirmed, we are given a reprise of what we learned earlier: God spoke to Moses in Egypt, giving him the commission to go to Pharaoh. Moses responded with the "I'm unskilled in speech" objection[3] (6:28–7:4).

God previously said He would make Moses "as God to Pharaoh" with Aaron as the spokesman (4:16). Here in Exodus 7:1 the LORD refers to Aaron as "your prophet."[4] The elder brother will serve as Moses' spokesman but fundamentally Aaron will speak the words of the LORD in pronouncing divine judgment on Egypt.

---

2 The groundwork is laid for Aaron and his offspring to be elevated at Mount Sinai to the office of Israel's High Priest in Exodus 28:1.

3 Compare the earlier narratives in Exodus 3:6-4:17 and 6:1–8.

4 This is the second mention of "prophet" (Hebrew *navi*) in Scripture; God gives Abraham that designation in Genesis 20:7. The office of prophet includes the concept of "forthtelling" as well as "foretelling" as God's representative on earth.

God also reiterates that He will harden Pharaoh's heart.[5] Pharaoh will only let Israel go under compulsion, the result of God's sign judgments.[6] Here God adds "and My wonders" – the first reference in the Bible to His miraculous portents. Indeed, a clear inference may be drawn from the text that the purpose of Pharaoh's heart being hardened is to provide opportunity for the Almighty to display His power.

Why all this drama?

The Creator has no need to "show off" His abilities. Indeed, Psalm 19 proclaims:

*1 The heavens are telling of the glory of God;
And their expanse is declaring the work of His hands.
2 Day to day pours forth speech,
And night to night reveals knowledge.
3 There is no speech, nor are there words;
Their voice is not heard.
4 Their line has gone out through all the earth,
And their utterances to the end of the world.*

What then is the purpose of the protracted showdown God is arranging? He states in Exodus 7:

4 "When Pharaoh does not listen to you, then I will lay My hand on Egypt and bring out My hosts, My people the sons of Israel, from the land of Egypt by great judgments. 5 The Egyptians

---

5 Exodus 7:4; see 4:21.

6 Exodus 7:1–3; see 3:19–20.

> *shall know that I am the LORD, when I stretch*
> *out My hand on Egypt and bring out the sons of*
> *Israel from their midst."*

In Exodus 6:7 we heard God express His intention that Israel *"shall know that I am the LORD"* – a statement He will repeat four more times in Exodus.[7] In 7:5 we learn the reason for God's "great judgments": *"The Egyptians shall know that I am the LORD."*[8]

"As the LORD commanded"

"So Moses and Aaron did it; as the LORD commanded them, thus they did" (7:6). Would this not be a desirable epitaph on one's tombstone? "He did what God commanded."

In the verse which follows we learn the brothers' ages when they marched into Pharaoh's office: Moses was 80, and Aaron, 83.

Not only is "retirement" not in the Bible, Moses and Aaron illustrate what God can do with octogenarians willing to do His bidding!

---

7   That God wants the Jewish people to know Him is a recurrent theme in the Tanakh (Old Testament). The densest concentration is in Ezekiel, where God says "that you may know that I am the LORD" 38 times to the nation or a subset thereof (e.g., "My people," "the house of Israel," "Jerusalem," and "the prophets").

8   This phrase will be repeated in Exodus 14:4 and 18. In Ezekiel, God says to/ about Egypt "that you/Egypt may know that I am the LORD" an additional seven times – further underscoring His desire that the Egyptian people know the true and living God.

Fear factor/Misery index

The children of Israel remain disillusioned and in bitter bondage; the hope of redemption has eluded them. The Egyptians continue in the position of power and authority over God's people. But the promised divine "signs and wonders" have the added ominous portent of "great judgments" to come.

Where is God?

God continues speaking to Moses and Aaron, revealing more of both His plan and His purpose. Specifically, the LORD is a "missionary God"; He wants to be known in a personal way and is about to demonstrate the lengths to which He will go to accomplish that end.

Chapter 16

The Power Encounter Begins

Exodus 7:8–25

God has already stated to Moses that He is going to manifest His signs and wonders such that both Israel and the Egyptians "will know that I am the LORD." But He has one more particular audience in mind as He displays His power.

Snakes alive!

The LORD has previously established the pattern that will be followed as our story unfolds. He tells Moses what to do and say.

Often included in God's instruction is insight into how Pharaoh will respond. He even anticipates what the Egyptian king will say. *"When Pharaoh speaks to you, saying, 'Work a miracle' ..."* (7:8–9).

Moses and Aaron make their second visit to Pharaoh, who sees a demonstration of God's power for the first time. Apparently, the king has been entertained by magic tricks previously. He summons his wise men, sorcerers, and magicians, who duplicate the "stick into serpent" routine with their "secret arts." But Aaron's serpent devours theirs! (7:10–12).

"Yet Pharaoh's heart was hardened,[1] *and he did not listen to them, as the LORD had said"*[2] (7:13).

Plague 1: Water to blood

We don't have a record of what Moses and Aaron discussed upon exiting Pharaoh's office. Perhaps it sounded like a resigned, "Well, that didn't work."

But God's plan is only in its beginning stages. He acknowledges the reality that *"Pharaoh's heart is stubborn"*[3] but instructs Moses to intercept the king at the Nile River in the morning.

> *16 You shall say to him, 'The LORD, the God of the Hebrews, sent me to you, saying, "Let My people go, that they may serve Me in the wilderness. But behold, you have not listened until now." 17 Thus*

1 This is the first time we see Pharaoh with a hardened heart. Though God had previously said He would harden the king's heart (4:21; 7:3), in this instance He is not stated to be the "hardening agent." The "God's sovereignty vs. man's free will" debate has raged for millennia. See Romans 9:14–24 for insight.

2 "[Just] as the LORD had said" is recurring reminder of God's foreknowledge in Scripture.

3 The Hebrew word *kaved* is most often translated "heavy," but has a wide range of meanings, such as "thick." In English we speak of people being "heavy-hearted" when sad or "thick-headed" when stubborn. Here "thick-hearted" equals obstinate.

says the LORD, "By this you shall know that I am the LORD: behold, I will strike the water that is in the Nile with the staff that is in my hand, and it will be turned to blood. 18 The fish that are in the Nile will die, and the Nile will become foul, and the Egyptians will find difficulty in drinking water from the Nile."'

Remember Pharaoh's response when Moses and Aaron first showed up as God's spokesmen? Pharaoh's first response was, *"Who is the LORD that I should obey His voice ...? I do not know the LORD"* (5:2).

Pharaoh still isn't listening. But God has more in mind than dialogue. What He had been intending to do all along He now explicitly states: *"By this you [Pharaoh]*[4] *shall know that I am the LORD"*[5] (7:17). The Nile will be turned to blood.

Moses passes along God's detailed instructions to Aaron, who raises his staff over the waters of Egypt. Rivers, streams, pools, and reservoirs (including the water in stone and wood storage containers) were turned to blood throughout all the land of Egypt. The fish all died; no water fit to drink remained (7:19–21).

Hard hearts don't easily move

Pharaoh's magicians use their secret arts to change water into blood. But what does that avail? The blood remains,

---

4 "You" is in the singular form here.

5 This is the first of six times God will say "that you may know" to Pharaoh; see also 8:22; 9:14, 19; 10:2; 11:7. Moses also says it to him in 9:29.

and the Egyptians now are forced to perform their own labor: digging wells to find water to drink.

A second time we read, "Pharaoh's heart was hardened, and he didn't listen to them, as the LORD had said" (7:22). Egypt's powerful ruler heads back to his house, unmoved and unconcerned about the devastating effects of this first plague.

Fear factor/Misery index

Until now, the situation has been intolerable for the suffering Hebrew slaves. Though Pharaoh shrugs off this first blow from God's hand, he is about to experience increasing discomfort.

Where is God?

For Moses, the LORD is both present and active, first person. Pharaoh is hearing God's words secondhand but he and everyone in Egypt are experiencing His judgment up close and personal.

And God? He takes a week's break (7:25).

Chapter 17

"No God Like Our God"

Exodus 8:1–15

After a week to think things over, Pharaoh has another chance to listen to the LORD's command. Will anything be different this time?

Plague 2: Frogs

The same LORD chooses the same emissary, Moses, to deliver the same message to the same Pharaoh. "Let My people go that they may serve/worship Me" (8:1).

As before, the command is accompanied by the threat of judgment – not blood this time, but frogs.

> *2 But if you refuse to let them go, behold, I will smite your whole territory with frogs. 3 The Nile will swarm with frogs, which will come up and go into your house and into your bedroom and*

on your bed, and into the houses of your servants
and on your people, and into your ovens and into
your kneading bowls. 4 So the frogs will come up
on you and your people and all your servants.

When warning of the first plague, God gave a general description (the Nile will become blood and fish will die). He provides much greater detail when depicting the second: frogs in your bed, frogs in your oven, frogs in your dishes. One need not have an overly vivid imagination to get a shiver down the spine.

At Moses' command, Aaron stretches out the staff over Egypt's water sources. The rivers, streams and pools which a week earlier had been filled with blood now teem with frogs (8:5–6).

As with the previous signs the magicians mimicked, so here. More frogs are made to appear[1] (8:7).

A breakthrough!

And Pharaoh? What's this? He summons Moses and Aaron back to the court. *"Entreat the LORD that He remove the frogs from me and from my people; and I will let the people go, that they may sacrifice to the LORD"* (8:8).

Moses even offers the king the honor of choosing the date when he would like the frogs to return to the Nile (8:9).

---

1 It's not a stretch to imagine those living in Egypt would have been much happier had the sorcerers made the frogs disappear – a power they evidently did not possess.

When Pharaoh chooses "tomorrow," Moses lets him know why he had been given the choice. *"May it be according to your word, that you may know that there is no one like the LORD our God"* (8:10–11).

Here Moses demonstrates his understanding of God's purpose for these demonstrations of power. The God of Israel is qualitatively different from the array of deities the Egyptians worshiped, and Pharaoh has a front row seat to see the mighty signs, wonders, and judgments of the LORD.

Interceding for Egypt

Having left Pharaoh's presence, Moses *"cried to the LORD concerning the frogs which He had inflicted upon Pharaoh"* (8:12). Why did he do this?

Of note, Pharaoh had requested Moses to *"entreat the LORD that He may remove the frogs ..."* (8:8).

Moses then asked Pharaoh, *"When shall I entreat for you and your servants and your people that the frogs be destroyed ...?"* (8:9). In encouraging the ruler of Egypt to "pick a date," Moses made it clear Whose power was at work. He was willing to seek God's favor on behalf of the Egyptians – and did so.

> *13 "The LORD did according to the word of Moses,*[2] *and the frogs died out of the houses, the*

---

2 We've seen a couple of times already that Moses and Aaron "did just as the LORD commanded them." Here we find the LORD doing "according to the word of Moses."

courts, and the fields. 14 So they piled them in heaps, and the land became foul" (8:13–14).

A change of heart?

Are we surprised to learn, *"But when Pharaoh saw that there was relief, he hardened his heart and did not listen to them, as the LORD had said"* (8:15)?

The king is not quoted saying, "I've changed my mind." But for the first time the statement is made, *"he hardened his heart."*[3]

Fear factor/Misery index

We see a "chink in Pharaoh's armor" as he momentarily relents[4] regarding releasing Israel for a wilderness worship service. Though the text provides no feedback from the Egyptian people, the description of the land being fouled by piles of decomposing frogs is enough to make one queasy. And this within a week of their waters being transformed into blood.

Where is God?

"As the LORD had said" at the close of Plague #2 reminds us that from heaven's perspective, everything is quite

---

3 God had said He would harden Pharaoh's heart, and twice we've seen the passive description: "Pharaoh's heart was hardened." Now we've come full circle and see clearly that Pharaoh is acting as a "free moral agent." He changed his mind because he hardened his heart.

4 One wonders if this could have been due more to the wailing of Mrs. Pharaoh reacting to a bedroom and kitchen full of slimy frogs than fear of the Almighty.

under control. That God was pleased to answer Moses' plea when God's glory was the prophet's highest goal should not be lost on us. Within the limitations of His holy character, there is no end to which God will not go for the glory of His own name.

Chapter 18
Swarming Insects, Bargaining Pharaoh

Exodus 8:16–32

Pharaoh's heart was hardened after Plague #1 (water to blood). He hardened his heart after Plague #2 (frogs everywhere). What's next?

Plague 3: "Itching to scratch"

God now instructs Moses to have Aaron strike the dust on the ground with the staff. What results is an annoying swarm of insects.[1] *"All the dust of the earth became gnats through all the land of Egypt"* (8:16–17). People and animals alike were afflicted.

---

1 These little critters, *kinim* in Hebrew, are variously identified as lice, sand flies, mosquitos, or more frequently, gnats. Regardless, they'd be unwelcome in one's home, clothing, hair, etc.

The finger of God

Once again the sorcerers seek to employ their magic arts to replicate the wonder. This time they fail. No turning dust into gnats – and certainly no getting rid of them from man nor beast.

Wouldn't it be interesting to know what the Egyptian magicians were thinking when they duplicated the early signs Aaron had performed (even though their serpent-staffs were eaten by his)? But they have reached the limitations of their secret arts. *Then the magicians said to Pharaoh, "This is the finger of God"* (8:19a).

Sadly, we read again, *Pharaoh's heart was hardened, and he did not listen to them, as the LORD had said* (8:19b).

Plague 4: Flies

As with the first plague, God instructs Moses to meet Pharaoh early in the morning on his bathing run to the Nile. The "fourth verse is the same as the first": *"Let My people go, that they may serve Me"* (8:20).

The consequences for disobedience are spelled out: If you don't send forth My people, I will send forth[2] swarming (and likely, biting) flies. And as with the second plague of frogs, God informs Pharaoh that he, his servants, his people and their houses – and even the ground – will suffer from this insect invasion.

---

2 The same Hebrew verb for "send/send out" is used for both actions.

A divine distinction

Now a new wrinkle is added, however:

> *22 "But on that day I will set apart the land of Goshen, where My people are living, so that no swarms of flies will be there, in order that you may know that I, the LORD, am in the midst of the land. 23 I will put a division between My people and your people. Tomorrow this sign will occur."*

The Hebrews living in Goshen have not been spared the ills of the first three plagues. That is about to change; the LORD will not send the flies among His people. And the purpose for doing so is clear: that Pharaoh will recognize that the LORD is present in their midst.

Pharaoh has but one day to obey. He does not, so the flies descend – on his house and on the Egyptian people. And lest we have the impression this is simply an annoyance, we are told *"the land was laid waste because of the swarms of flies in all the land of Egypt"* (8:24).

"Let's make a deal"

The ruler of Egypt has had enough.

Well, almost. The initial request was for a three-day journey into the wilderness for a worship service (5:1–3.) That's not going to happen anytime soon, according to Pharaoh's thinking. But he does make an offer: *"Go, sacrifice to your God within the land"* (8:25).

Moses explains why this is not a great idea, citing not wanting to offend the Egyptians, who would observe and object to the Hebrews' sacrifices. And besides, God commanded them to journey three days into the desert (8:26–27).

Pharaoh counters with an okay to go to the wilderness to sacrifice, but "don't go very far." And adds, *"Make supplication for me"* (8:28).

Moses agrees to pray for the flies to disappear the next day. He concludes with a warning. *"Only do not let Pharaoh deal deceitfully again in not letting the people go to sacrifice to the LORD"* (8:29).

No surprise ending here

Moses prays. God answers, *"doing as Moses asked."* The swarms of insects are gone; *"not one remained"* (8:30–31).

> *But Pharaoh hardened his heart this time also, and he did not let the people go* (8:32).

Fear factor/Misery index

Flies can be pesky, buzzing about one's face. Flies can be nasty, spreading disease. Biting flies can inflict real pain. But as bad as any negative experience you or I have had with swarming insects, Plague #4 tops it by far.

Where is God?

For the first time we see the light dawning among the Egyptians. *"This is the finger of God"* (8:19) is the testimony of Pharaoh's "power brokers" who recognize that something beyond magic or sorcery is at work here.

And the Hebrews, whose suffering has continued, are now catching a break. The God of Israel is distinguishing His people from the Egyptians.

The Creator's *"that you may know that I am the LORD"* agenda is beginning to have an effect!

Chapter 19

Disease, Boils and Hail – Oh My!

Exodus 9:1–35

Egypt has endured four plagues, the first three of which also affected the Jewish people in Goshen. But God is making a distinction between the Egyptians and Hebrews so that everyone (especially Pharaoh) will know the LORD. Pharaoh's heart remains hard – so life is about to get harder.

Plague 5: Cattle disease

Nothing is impossible for the Creator who speaks worlds into existence. Think of the ways in which He could have instantaneously released the Jewish people from their bondage. Instead, we have a protracted series of plagues – because God has a global agenda.

In Exodus 9, Moses' warning to Pharaoh of the impending fifth plague indicated how widespread the pestilence would be:

> *"Let My people go, that they may serve Me. 2 For if you refuse to let them go and continue to hold them, 3 behold, the hand of the LORD will come with a very severe pestilence on your livestock which are in the field, on the horses, on the donkeys, on the camels, on the herds, and on the flocks."*

As with the previous plague, a "one-day notice"[1] is issued, along with the clarification that the Hebrew's livestock would not be affected. And, true to His word, the next day **all the livestock of Egypt died; but of the livestock of the sons of Israel, not one died** (9:6).

Pharaoh investigates and confirms the truth of God's promise. But his heart is hardened and the Hebrews are not released to worship the LORD.

Plague 6: Boils

The sixth plague gets comparatively little fanfare. At God's instruction, Moses and Aaron toss soot into the sky in front of Pharaoh. Result: Man and beast are covered with boils (9:8–10).

This time the court magicians cannot show up to mimic the miracle. Their boils are too painful. And for the first

---

1 "The LORD set a definite time" (9:5) is a clear reminder that God's plan includes specific timing.

time we find the LORD as the agent of hardening in Pharaoh's heart (9:11–12).

Plague 7: Hail

Early in the morning Moses confronts Pharaoh. First comes the rebuke:

> **14 *"For this time I will send all My plagues on you and your servants and your people, so that you may know that there is no one like Me in all the earth. 15 For if by now I had put forth My hand and struck you and your people with pestilence, you would then have been cut off from the earth. 16 But, indeed, for this reason I have allowed you to remain, in order to show you My power and in order to proclaim My name through all the earth."***

Notice of the impending plague soon follows. "You think you've seen hailstorms before? Tomorrow you'll experience the worst in Egyptian history. Believe me, and you'll bring whatever remains of your livestock to shelter. Don't believe Me, and you'll pay the price" is the basic warning.

Sure enough, the next day *the LORD sent thunder and hail, and fire ran down to the earth* (9:23a). The severity of the storm flattened plants and shattered trees throughout Egypt – but Goshen was spared (9:25–26).

Pharaoh repents – almost

This "triple whammy" of plagues (against livestock, humans, and plant life) finally brings Pharaoh to admit he's had enough. He confesses to Moses and Aaron, *"I have sinned this time; the LORD is the righteous one, and I and my people are the wicked ones"* (9:27–28).

He asks Moses to pray for an end to the horrific storm. Moses agrees, reminding Pharaoh this is so he may know the earth belongs to the LORD. Because Moses understands, *"But as for you and your servants, I know that you do not yet fear the LORD God"* (9:29–30).

True to his character, when Pharaoh sees the storm stop, *he sinned again and hardened his heart, he and his servants. Pharaoh's heart was hardened,*[2] *and he did not let the sons of Israel go, just as the LORD had spoken through Moses* (9:34–35).

2 Pharaoh's "sclerosis of the heart" is described in three ways: "Pharaoh hardened his heart"; "Pharaoh's heart was hardened" (passive voice); and "the LORD hardened Pharaoh's heart." Usually only one form is used, but all three are found immediately following Plague #7. Here is the full sequence, including future plagues:

a. God states He will harden Pharaoh's heart – 4:21 and 7:3.
b. Plague #1: Blood – Pharaoh's heart was hardened (7:13 and 7:22; and God says Pharaoh's heart is "heavy/thick" in 7:14).
c. Plague #2: Frogs – Pharaoh hardened his heart (8:15).
d. Plague #3 Gnats – Pharaoh's heart was hardened (8:19).
e. Plague #4: Flies – Pharaoh hardened his heart (8:32).
f. Plague #5: Cattle disease – Pharaoh's heart was hardened (9:7).
g. Plague #6: Boils – God hardened Pharaoh's heart (9:12).
h. Plague #7: Hail – Pharaoh hardened his heart (9:34); Pharaoh's heart was hardened (9:35); God hardened Pharaoh's heart (10:1).
i. Plague #8: Locusts – God hardened Pharaoh's heart (10:20).
j. Plague #9: Darkness – God hardened Pharaoh's heart (10:27 and 11:10).
k. Plague #10: Firstborn son dies – God hardened Pharaoh's heart (14:4); Pharaoh has "a change (lit. 'overturn') of heart" (14:5); God hardened Pharaoh's heart (14:8 and 14:17).

Fear factor/Misery index

Experiencing COVID-19 in 2020 brought a fresh realization to many of the terror a pandemic can cause. It took a terrible toll in lives and the economy; the restrictions placed on individuals caused massive change to daily life. Consider the resources expended to combat one small virus. Then multiply that by the intensity, severity, and scope of the seven plagues God has unleashed on Egypt thus far.

Where is God?

"Why does God allow the wicked to prosper (or even draw breath)?" is an age-old question. In this passage of Scripture we see heaven's perspective. The LORD has a wider agenda than deposing a petty potentate; in essence He tells the king of Egypt, "I didn't just strike you dead immediately because the whole world is going to hear about My unleashed power and know that I am the LORD."

We see success in God's purposes among the Egyptians who *feared the word of the LORD*; they heeded the warning and drove their livestock to shelter (9:20).

In Exodus we have one of the most visible demonstrations of the LORD acting in history. He foretells what He will do, He does it, and He tells us why. Our challenge in difficult times is to remember God is always at work, whether He tells us His plan or not.

As Babbie Mason sings, "God is too good to be unkind and He is too wise to be mistaken. And when we cannot trace His hand, we must trust His heart."[3]

3 The lyrics to Mason's "Trust His Heart" comes from a common paraphrase of Charles Spurgeon's sermon "A Happy Christian," in which he stated, "[the Christian] … believes [God] to be too wise to err and too good to be unkind; he trusts Him where he cannot trace Him, looks up to Him in the darkest hour, and believes that all is well."

Chapter 20

Never So Many Again

Exodus 10:1–20

The pattern is now well-established: God speaks to Moses; Moses tells Pharaoh what will happen; Pharaoh doesn't listen; God sends a plague. And then another.

Plague 8: Locusts

Here in Exodus 10 we once again see Moses and Aaron approach Pharaoh with a word from the God of Israel:

> *3 "How long will you refuse to humble yourself before Me? Let My people go, that they may serve Me. 4 For if you refuse to let My people go, behold, tomorrow I will bring locusts into your territory. 5 They shall cover the surface of the land, so that no one will be able to see the land. They will also eat the rest of what has escaped—what is left to you from the hail—and they will eat every tree*

which sprouts for you out of the field. 6 Then your houses shall be filled and the houses of all your servants and the houses of all the Egyptians, something which neither your fathers nor your grandfathers have seen, from the day that they came upon the earth until this day."

Pharaoh's servants have seen the pattern played out seven times already. They have observed God's power displayed over and over, with grave consequences to their land and possessions. "Enough already! Just let them go worship the LORD their God, will you? Can't you see that Egypt is devastated?" they plead with their sovereign (10:7).

Moses and Aaron are called back to the throne. Pharaoh is prepared to negotiate. "Okay, you may leave. But only the men. Women and children must remain. Now, get out of here."

At the LORD's command, Moses stretches out his trusty staff. The east wind begins to blow all day and throughout the night, and with it come the hordes.

14 The locusts came up over all the land of Egypt and settled in all the territory of Egypt; they were very numerous. There had never been so many locusts, nor would there be so many again. 15 For they covered the surface of the whole land, so that the land was darkened; and they ate every plant of the land and all the fruit of the trees that the hail had left. Thus nothing green was

*left on tree or plant of the field through all the
land of Egypt.*

Pharaoh repents again – almost

Unlike the early plagues in which Pharaoh seems almost
leisurely in responding to God's judgment, he now
summons Moses and Aaron in a hurry.

> *16 "I have sinned against the LORD your God and
> against you. 17 Now therefore, please forgive my
> sin only this once, and make supplication to the
> LORD your God, that He would only remove this
> death from me" (10:16c–17).*

Moses prays. God sends a west wind to blow away every
last locust from Egypt. The Israelites remain in Goshen,
untouched by the locusts (10:18–19).

And God hardens Pharaoh's heart (10:20).

Fear factor/Misery index

If you've seen video of the massive swarms of locusts
in eastern Africa, perhaps you shuddered to see the
devastation they cause. The sky and ground are black
with them. They multiply quickly, move swiftly, and
leave nothing green behind.

Now imagine the Egyptians who have already endured
seven plagues which have left them reeling, destitute,
and hurting.

Where is God?

Let's return to the beginning of chapter 10. God tells Moses He has hardened the hearts of Pharaoh and his servants *"that I may perform these signs of Mine among them, 2 and that you may tell in the hearing of your son, and of your grandson, how I made a mockery of the Egyptians and how I performed My signs among them, that you may know that I am the LORD"* (vv. 1–2).

We have the direct statement of the LORD that one of the purposes of this protracted display of divine power is that the generations that follow may hear of God's exploits. The generation of Moses' grandparents and great-grandparents endured great suffering without seeing deliverance by the God of their fathers.

The generations which followed the Exodus would not experience the concentrated array of judgments on the enemies of the Jewish people. Though God remains in "the miracle-working business," few have seen divine power on display[1] over and over on such a grand scale.

One of the greatest challenges in the family of faith is passing the torch to the next generation. Moses would

---

1 We have the record of Creation (Was there ever such a display of omnipotence as when the LORD spoke the universe into existence, set the Earth on its orbit around the sun, and spun the DNA of every living creature?). But no human eye beheld any of this; Adam and Eve were the culmination of creation. Apart from the miracles recorded in the life of Moses, we have only two other times in Scripture when God's power was repeatedly demonstrated in individual's lives: Elijah/Elisha and Yeshua (Jesus of Nazareth). The book of Revelation tells us of the coming "last days" when the greatest concentration of God's judgments will be poured out on Earth's wicked inhabitants.

later pass on these instructions to the children of the Exodus:

> *4 "Hear, O Israel! The LORD is our God, the LORD is one! 5 You shall love the LORD your God with all your heart and with all your soul and with all your might. 6 These words, which I am commanding you today, shall be on your heart. 7 You shall teach them diligently to your sons and shall talk of them when you sit in your house and when you walk by the way and when you lie down and when you rise up. 8 You shall bind them as a sign on your hand and they shall be as frontals on your forehead. 9 You shall write them on the doorposts of your house and on your gates"* (Deuteronomy 6:4–9).

We have seen repeatedly how Pharaoh was remorseful but not truly repentant. As soon as his circumstances improved, he didn't need to deal with God any longer (or so he thought).

What about us? We cry out for deliverance in tough times, for sure. But when God brings us through, what then? It's instructive to see how Moses continues his exhortation in Deuteronomy 6:

> *10 "Then it shall come about when the LORD your God brings you into the land which He swore to your fathers, Abraham, Isaac and Jacob, to give you, great and splendid cities which you did not build, 11 and houses full of all good things which you did not fill, and hewn cisterns which you did*

not dig, vineyards and olive trees which you did not plant, and you eat and are satisfied, 12 then watch yourself, that you do not forget the LORD who brought you from the land of Egypt, out of the house of slavery" (vv. 10–12).

Perhaps this is a good day to tell your kids and grandkids the stories of your experiences of God's guarding, guiding, and providing in your life.

Chapter 21
Lights Out and Last Chance

Throughout the land of Egypt, water sources have been polluted. Homes filled with frogs and bugs. Crops and livestock wiped out. Bodies blistered with festering boils. The worst thunderstorm in Egypt's recorded history terrorized the populace as hailstones pelted down. The citizens are ready for these recurring nightmares to end. But Pharaoh has a heart problem.

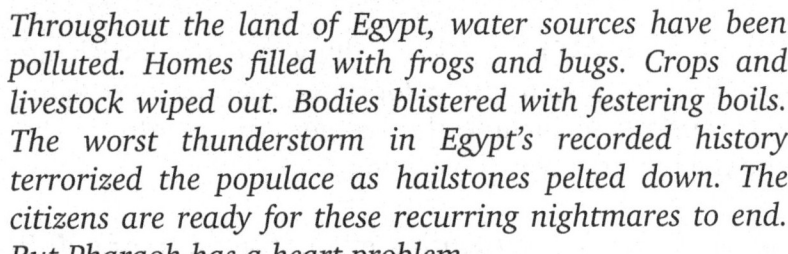

Plague 9: Darkness

No one is comfortable very long not being able to see their hands in front of their faces, literally. It's one thing to willingly experience temporary blindness, and quite another to have *a darkness that may be felt* inflicted for three days (10:21–22).

Those enduring isolation caused by the novel coronavirus know what it means to "shelter in place." Imagine doing so in a world gone dark. No dawn, sunlight, or twilight. No moon or twinkling stars. *They did not see one another, nor did anyone rise from his place for three days, but all the sons of Israel had light in their dwellings* (10:23).

No mention is made of Egypt's wise men here. World-class astrologers, these observers knew the heavens well. Eclipses could be explained; three days of total "lights out" could not. Especially when neighboring Goshen had light.

Pharaoh relents – almost

After Plague #8 Pharaoh was willing to let the Jewish men go off to worship in the wilderness. Now he's extending the reprieve to include the women and children – but the flocks and herds must remain.

Moses is not in a negotiating mood. *"Not a hoof will be left behind"* (10:25–26).

God is not finished with Pharaoh just yet. He hardens the king's heart (10:27).

And hardened it is. Pharaoh tells Moses, *"Get away from me! Beware, do not see my face again, for in the day you see my face you shall die!"* (10:28).

Moses responds, *"You are right; I shall never see your face again!"* (10:29).

But the LORD has one more message for Pharaoh ...

"I'm going on a trip ..."

Since God appeared to Moses at the burning bush, He has been instructing His servant, preparing him for what lay ahead. Nine plagues have passed. Pharaoh has bent, but not broken.

Now the LORD lets Moses know that the end is in sight. *"One more plague I will bring on Pharaoh and on Egypt; after that he will let you go from here. When he lets you go, he will surely drive you out from here completely"* (11:1).

God goes on to remind[1] Moses to instruct the children of Israel upon their departure to ask their Egyptian neighbors for assistance. They are not just to ask for a sack lunch for their journey. They are to fill their sacks with *articles of silver and articles of gold* (11:2).

A change of heart

The LORD gave the people favor in the sight of the Egyptians. Furthermore, the man Moses himself was greatly esteemed in the land of Egypt, both in the sight of Pharaoh's servants and in the sight of the people (11:3).

1 Long before Joseph was sold into Egyptian slavery, the LORD promised Abraham that after his descendants had been enslaved and oppressed 400 years in a land not their own, they would "come out with many possessions" (Genesis 15:13–14). Along with His initial instructions to Moses at the burning bush was God's promise that He would grant the Jewish people favor in the sight of the Egyptians so they would not leave empty-handed. In addition to silver and gold, clothing would also be given freely (3:21–22).

What a difference a plague (or nine) makes! From despised slaves to finding favor with their oppressors is quite a change in status. Notably, just as the LORD had been at work hardening hearts of Pharaoh's servants (10:1), He now softens them.

The final warning

But there is one heart that hasn't softened: Pharaoh's. The text does not record the details of when and where Moses had his final encounter with the Egyptian king (who had promised to kill him if Moses showed his face again). But the script for the last plague had been dictated by God back in the wilderness of Midian.

> *21 "When you go back to Egypt see that you perform before Pharaoh all the wonders which I have put in your power; but I will harden his heart so that he will not let the people go. 22 Then you shall say to Pharaoh, 'Thus says the LORD, "Israel is My son, My firstborn. 23 So I said to you, 'Let My son go that he may serve Me'; but you have refused to let him go. Behold, I will kill your son, your firstborn"'"* (4:21–23).

Up till now the Egyptians had suffered physical pain and fiscal loss. They had seen piles of dead frogs and livestock. With God's final judgment, humans would die – and not just Pharaoh's son:

> *5 "And all the firstborn in the land of Egypt shall die, from the firstborn of the Pharaoh who sits on his throne, even to the firstborn of the slave girl who is behind the millstones; all the firstborn of*

the cattle as well. 6 Moreover, there shall be a great cry in all the land of Egypt, such as there has not been before and such as shall never be again" (11:5–6).

The last shall be first

Our study in Exodus began with the enslavement of the Hebrews and Pharaoh's edict to kill their baby boys. The Jewish people sighed, cried, and groaned because of their bondage and ill treatment.

The story has now come full circle. It is the Egyptians who will soon be wailing in anguish. *"But against any of the sons of Israel a dog will not even bark, whether against man or beast, that you may understand how the LORD makes a distinction between Egypt and Israel"* (11:7).

Moses informs Pharaoh that his servants who have always prostrated themselves before him will soon be bowing down to Moses. They finally will insist that Moses depart with his people, *"and after that I will go out"* (11:8). Then Moses departed from Pharaoh "with his nose on fire."[2]

Pharaoh will not listen

Are we surprised when God tells Moses that Pharaoh will not change? Once more He reveals His purpose in

---

2 In English we say, "His face flushed with anger." The Hebrew idiom is "His nose burned." Moses has had enough of Pharaoh's stubborn pride and unwillingness to submit to the LORD.

hardening Pharaoh's heart: *"so that My wonders will be multiplied in the land of Egypt"* (11:9–10).

Fear factor/Misery index

Darkness is a source of primal fear beginning in early childhood. Even adults get the shivers when we can't see what's out there at night.

Pharaoh's stress level has hit the max. Still operating as though he is in control, he promised if he saw Moses again, he'd kill him. Of course, that was not God's plan.

The Egyptians are more than ready for the Hebrews to depart.

Where is God?

On time and on target, the Sovereign of the Universe continues to orchestrate events. His four-century plan as revealed to Abraham includes an 80-year-old Jewish man whose life was spared from a death sentence as an infant. The nation comprised of Jacob's offspring has multiplied. As God's firstborn, they are about to be redeemed by His mighty hand and outstretched arm.

Chapter 22

"I will pass over you"

Exodus 12:1–28

God's countdown from 10 has reached number 1. Pharaoh has been warned of the impending judgment of the God of Israel. Every firstborn male, from the palace to the servant's quarters and in the pasture as well, will be struck dead. But first, the LORD has a final set of instructions for the Jewish people.

A new calendar

Great empires have a way of seeing history through very parochial eyes. For example, Year 1 on the Roman calendar (753 BC on the Gregorian calendar used widely today) began with the founding of the city of Rome (*Ab urbe condita or AUC*).

We may suppose the Jewish people had grown accustomed to the Egyptian calendar tracking the dynasties of the pharaohs. Now God is going to institute a new way for His people to mark time: *"This month shall be the beginning of months for you; it is to be the first month of the year to you"* (12:2).

The LORD continues with very specific instructions:

> Count 10 days into this first month on your new calendar. Every family must select an unblemished year-old lamb or goat. Observe it for four days to be certain it has no illness or defect.

> At twilight on the 14th of the month everyone is to kill their lamb and collect the blood in a basin. Some of that blood must be applied with a hyssop branch to the doorposts and lintel of each home. Roast the lamb over fire and eat it, along with unleavened bread and bitter herbs, at home with your family. But eat quickly, ready to leave at a moment's notice (12:1–11, paraphrased).

Pretty strange way to prepare a meal before a trip, we might think. But this is no ordinary going-away dinner; it is "the LORD's Passover."

"I will pass over you"

The sand in God's 400-year hourglass has run out. After generations of bitter bondage, the Hebrews are more than ready to leave Egypt. But Pharaoh is unrelenting in his stubborn refusal to release his slaves. So, God has one final plague to unleash on the Egyptians.

For I will go through the land of Egypt on that night, and will strike down all the firstborn in the land of Egypt, both man and beast; and against all the gods of Egypt I will execute judgments—I am the LORD (12:12).

Since the fourth plague, the God of Abraham has made a distinction between the Jewish people and the Egyptians, sparing Goshen from devastation. He intends to provide protection for them from the final judgment. But this time He requires action on their part: applying lamb's blood to the entrances of each family's home.

The blood shall be a sign for you on the houses where you live; and when I see the blood I will pass over you, and no plague will befall you to destroy you when I strike the land of Egypt (12:13).

A memorial Feast of Unleavened Bread

God will fill out the Jewish calendar with additional days of annual celebration and observance,[1] but Passover is the first to be initiated. A perpetual ordinance to be kept throughout ensuing generations; this is a memorial feast with specific elements. For seven days the Jewish people are to eat bread without leaven, recalling that when escaping Egypt there was no time for dough to rise. In fact, no leaven should be found in the house for that week (12:14–20).

---

1 See Leviticus 23 for the complete list of "God's appointed times." Purim was added to the calendar in the days of Esther and Mordechai to celebrate deliverance from Haman's evil plot to annihilate the Jewish people. Hanukkah (Feast of Dedication) occurs after the closing of the Tanakh; it is mentioned in John 10:22.

To underscore the seriousness of this permanent regulation, God states (then reaffirms) that *"whoever eats what is leavened, that person shall be cut off from the congregation of Israel,²* *whether he is an alien or a native of the land"* (12:15, 19b).

Moses then passes on God's instructions to the elders of Israel, including the key element of putting lamb's blood on the entrances of their dwellings.

> *For the LORD will pass through to smite the Egyptians; and when He sees the blood on the lintel and on the two doorposts, the LORD will pass over the door and will not allow the destroyer³ to come in to your houses to smite you* (12:23).

The importance of understanding the significance of the LORD's redeeming His people from Egyptian bondage (by both observing the Feast of Unleavened Bread annually and retelling the story to future generations) is underscored throughout this text.

---

2 This is only the second time the Torah levies this serious punishment. The first time is for the failure to circumcise one's son, thus breaking God's covenant (17:14).

3 The Passover Haggadah emphasizes God's personal involvement in the slaying of the firstborn: "I Myself and not another." Our text (Exodus 12:23) indicates the LORD indeed will pass through to smite the Egyptians. It also references "the destroyer" whom He will not allow into the homes of the Hebrews to smite them. In 2 Samuel 24:15 we also see the LORD sending a pestilence (*dever*, the same word used of the fifth plague in Exodus 9:3) which killed 70,000 Israelites. 2 Samuel 24:16–17 refers to "the angel who destroyed the people" and "the Angel of the LORD" – the same language used of the divine appearance at the burning bush. Some connect these two passages to identify "the destroyer" of Exodus 3 to be the angel of the LORD as the instrument of divine judgment.

> *"... You shall say [to your children who inquire], 'It is a Passover sacrifice to the LORD who passed over the houses of the sons of Israel in Egypt when He smote the Egyptians, but spared our homes'"* (12:27).

The Jewish people responded to Moses by bowing and worshiping the LORD. They then *went and did so; just as the LORD had commanded Moses and Aaron, so they did* (12:28). Faith in action – worship and obedience – would bring deliverance from death for the firstborn of the Hebrews.

Fear factor/Misery index

After all the years of sighing and crying, toiling and boiling in the North African sun, the long nightmare of slavery is about to end. A final barbecue is planned, with a rather sparse menu. The meal must be eaten hurriedly because there is much to do before departing in the morning.

Was it a long or short night, huddled inside the home one last time? Were you the firstborn male in your family, would you have double-checked to make sure the blood had been daubed on the doorposts and lintel as instructed?

Where is God?

Exodus opens with the Hebrews in misery, crying out for relief. God seems absent, perhaps uncaring. After His demonstrations of divine power and the protection from Plague 4 onward for the Jewish people, we now find Him being worshiped.

And the Creator of the Universe is establishing the Jewish calendar to begin with the annual recounting of this amazing chapter of history so future generations will know Him as *"the LORD our God who brought us out of bondage in Egypt."*

Chapter 23
Free at Last!

Only those who have been held in captivity can truly appreciate freedom. Only the slave set free knows how precious emancipation is. The longsuffering Hebrews are about to taste those realities. But their story unfolds against an anguishing backdrop in Egypt.

A great cry in Egypt

> **29 Now it came about at midnight that the LORD struck all the firstborn in the land of Egypt, from the firstborn of Pharaoh who sat on his throne to the firstborn of the captive who was in the dungeon, and all the firstborn of cattle. 30 Pharaoh arose in the night, he and all his servants and all the Egyptians, and there was a great cry in Egypt, for there was no home where there was not someone dead** (12:29–30).

All life is precious. Every death is a cause for sorrow.[1]

Pharaoh's resolve

> *31 Then [Pharaoh] called for Moses and Aaron at night and said, "Rise up, get out from among my people, both you and the sons of Israel; and go, worship the LORD, as you have said. 32 Take both your flocks and your herds, as you have said, and go, and bless me also"* (12:31–32).

Think of the cost of Pharaoh's pride and unwillingness to listen to the words of God. Like a child whose fingers must be pried, one by one, from the cherished item he clings to, Pharaoh has repeatedly refused the direct order from God: "Let My people go!"

We see Pharaoh's progression from "No way you're leaving! Work harder!" to "The men can go – but only for three days" to "Okay, take the women and children – but no animals."

Now, he releases his hand – and the Jewish people. "Go away! Worship – as you have said. Take the livestock – as you have said. And say a prayer for me."

The Egyptian people are in full agreement that the Hebrews should leave as soon as possible. Otherwise, *"We shall all be dead"* (12:33).

---

1 The tradition of removing a drop of wine from our cups when each plague is recited during a Passover Seder reflects the idea of joy diminished by human suffering – even that of our enemies.

Time to go

Having eaten in haste their last meal as slaves, the Jewish people now leave in a hurry. They do not depart emptyhanded. The LORD's promise to give them favor in the eyes of the Egyptians was fulfilled. In addition to their unleavened bread and kneading bowls, the now-freed captives head east bearing silver and gold items along with the clothing the Egyptians contributed to the plunder (12:34–36).

We may consider the treasures taken out of Egypt as a form of compensation for the generations of slave labor the Jewish people contributed to Pharaoh's treasury and the Egyptian economy. But think of the resources that will be needed to clothe the priests in colorful robes and construct and outfit the tabernacle (e.g., lampstand and ark of the covenant made of gold) as detailed in Exodus 25–28. Where would slaves have found such resources in the desert?

Fear factor/Misery index

When tragedies such as pandemics, natural disasters, or terror attacks are unleashed, we are reminded of the uncertainty of life. Each time the death count mounts by one, the weight of grief increases for the deceased's family and friends.

Imagine if every home in our country experienced the loss of a loved one in a single night. The wave of mourning that would sweep through our communities would be overwhelming.

The economic devastation and disruption of daily life from the first nine plagues brought hardship and bitterness to the Egyptians – just as they had embittered the lives of the Hebrews. The sentence of death Pharaoh had ordered for the Hebrew baby boys is mirrored in the loss of his own firstborn son and in all the families of Egypt.

Where is God?

"Against all the gods of Egypt I will execute judgments" (12:12) is a phrase we ought not overlook. With over 2,000 named deities, it might be easier to list what the polytheistic Egyptians didn't worship than what they did. For example:

- The Nile River overflows its banks every spring, bringing fertility to the land, and thus was worshiped. God executed His judgment over the Nile god in Plague 1, turning what had been a source of life into polluted pools of blood.

- Mut, the mother goddess, was often depicted as a cow.[2] With the fifth plague wiping out Egypt's livestock, the LORD demonstrated His power over the cow god.

- The sun god, Ra, was Egypt's most powerful deity. With three days of total darkness, the ninth

---

2 Deeper into the Exodus saga God's "nose catches fire" in anger (32:10) when the Hebrews fashion a golden calf (doubtless from the donated plunder). Aaron heightens the blasphemy by announcing, "Tomorrow shall be a feast to the LORD" after the people said of the calf idol, "This is your god, O Israel, who brought you up from the land of Egypt" (32:1–8).

plague proved all celestial gods[3] powerless before the LORD.

- Pharaoh himself was worshiped as a deity. With the tenth plague God killed the "god in waiting" in the person of Pharaoh's firstborn son, heir to the Egyptian throne.

Here's a question for each of us to ponder: *What does it take for me to acknowledge the Sovereign of the Universe, to hear His voice, to trust in Him and walk in His paths?*

If you want more information about God's righteous requirements and provision for your redemption, read "Safe When the Deadly Plague Passes Over" at **www.insearchofshalom.com/blog/ safe-when-the-deadly-plague-passes-over**

Or scan this:

---

3 Ra was the "noon god," when the sun was at full strength; Horus was the sky god. Later in Egyptian history Ra was "rebranded" as Amun or Amun-Ra. One needs a thick "directory" to keep track of Egyptian deities.

Chapter 24
Lest We Forget

The tenth and final plague has left the Egyptians in deep mourning. In one night of God's judgment, the firstborn male in every household was struck dead. Pharaoh at last is willing to release the Jewish people, without restrictions. Laden with clothing, gold, and silver contributed by their neighbors, the Hebrews depart in haste.

Setting out from Egypt

Our narrator provides details that help us understand the scale of what God is doing. *37 Now the sons of Israel journeyed from Rameses to Succoth, about six hundred thousand men on foot, aside from children. 38 A mixed multitude also went up with them, along with flocks and herds, a very large number of livestock* (12:37–38).

In addition to the sizable Jewish contingent of men, women, and children, a large number of others of "foreign descent"[1] joined the exodus. In Exodus 7:5 God had said to the Egyptians *"that you may know that I am the LORD."* That so many of them joined the departing throng is a testimony to the effectiveness of the God of Israel's demonstrations of judgment upon the gods of Egypt.

We are reminded of the haste in which the departure took place. The bread was made without leaven *since they were driven out of Egypt and could not delay, nor had they prepared any provisions[2] for themselves* (12:39).

We also are given a time marker. It was *at the end of four hundred and thirty years, to the very day, that all the hosts of the LORD went out from the land of Egypt* (12:41).

A meal to remember

The first 27 verses of Exodus 12 contain God's instructions to His people regarding Passover. Included were the necessity of applying blood to the doorway and the commands regarding the perpetual celebration of the Feast of Unleavened Bread.

That Passover *is a night to be observed for LORD for having brought them out from the land of Egypt* is

1 The Egyptians who joined the throng of Hebrews represent millions of Gentiles who have benefited over the millennia from the LORD's promise to Abraham: "In you all the families of the earth will be blessed" (12:3).

2 The provisioning of this multitude would be a daunting challenge for any leader in the best of circumstances, much less in a desert setting.

emphasized by the repetition of "for the LORD." That it is *to be observed by all the sons of Israel throughout their generations* indicates the broad scope and lasting duration of the ordinance (12:42, 47).

God continues to provide clear guidelines for how Passover is to be kept, including:
- No foreigner, including sojourners or hired help, may participate (unless circumcised).[3]
- This is not a "moveable feast"; the meal must be eaten entirely in each Jewish home (12:46).

Obedience – and deliverance!

50 Then all the sons of Israel did so; they did just as the LORD had commanded Moses and Aaron. 51 And on that same day the LORD brought the sons of Israel out of the land of Egypt by their hosts (12:50–51).

No firstborn male died in a Hebrew home in Goshen. One may imagine the oldest son in every home who was old enough to understand the consequences of disobedience would have made sure the blood was properly applied to his front door.

Now after long years of hard labor and oppression the Jewish people were finally free – and heading home.

---

3 Exodus 12:42–45,48–49.

Fear factor/Misery index

No mention is made in this text of the emotional state of the Jewish people. In stark contrast to the bitter cries of grief of the Egyptians, each mourning a death in their home, the children of Israel likely were dealing with a roiling mixture of hope (*Can you believe it? We're finally getting out of here!*) with concern (*Pharaoh has changed his mind before. Will he really let us go this time?*).

Having hope amidst uncertainty can be considered "whistling in the dark" while wishing for the best. For the believer, it is a matter of the will to entrust our lives and loved ones to our all-wise and compassionate God. "I choose to trust You, Lord" is a fitting prayer in any circumstance.

Where is God?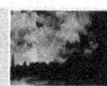

The LORD brought the sons of Israel out of the land of Egypt (12:51). Think of all that transpired from the time God told Moses He would deliver His people from bondage. We could have been given just the summary statement that He did so.

But the LORD is purposeful in all He does. The details of the unfolding plagues, Pharaoh's hardened heart, and the demonstrations of God's power over the gods of Egypt are included for our instruction. As is the reminder to remember, perpetually, what He has done for us.

God is in the details (even small ones)

Among the small details included in our text is the phrase *nor are you to break any bone of it* (12:46). Instructions given earlier in this chapter included selection of an unblemished year-old male lamb or goat on the 10th of the month to be sacrificed, roasted, and eaten on the 14th. But now the "don't break any bone" command is added. *Why is that?* we may wonder.

The answer is found when we learn Messiah was prefigured in the Passover. In the New Covenant we read, *For Messiah our Passover also has been sacrificed* (1 Corinthians 5:7). Here are some connecting points:

- The "Last Supper" of Yeshua (Jesus of Nazareth) with His disciples was a Passover meal.

- Psalm 22, written by King David about 1,000 years before Messiah came, includes:

  □ Yeshua's cry from the cross, *"My God, my God, why have You forsaken me?"* (verse 1).

  □ A depiction of the crowd of mockers who despised Him, taunting Him to call on God to rescue Him (verses 6–8).

  □ The description of physical suffering which parallels what those crucified[4] endured, including bones out of joint and great thirst (verses 14–15,17a).

---

4 Crucifixion was unknown at the time David wrote Psalm 22. Executing people on a cross was introduced by the Romans centuries later as a form of punishment and public example of what happened to enemies of the Empire.

- ☐ Pierced hands and feet, just as when a victim is nailed to a cross (verse 16).

- ☐ Lots were cast for his garment (verse 18), as was true for Yeshua.

- Though the thieves crucified on either side of Yeshua had their legs broken to hasten their deaths, the Roman soldier pierced Yeshua's side with a spear. Not one of His bones were broken.

- Just as God instructed the Jewish people to remember what He had done in redeeming Israel from bondage by retelling the Passover story annually, so Yeshua instructed His followers to remember Him through the bread and cup at the LORD's Supper.

- John the Baptizer had identified Yeshua as *"the Lamb of God who takes away the sin of the world"* as He began His public ministry (John 1:29).

Sometimes our God displays His power in ways visible to all, as in the judgments with which He struck Egypt. At other times His fingerprints are seen in the smallest of details. But He is always present and ever at work.

Chapter 25
A Dedication to Remember

Exodus 13:1–16

God has already instituted the annual celebration of Passover to memorialize deliverance from Egypt. The importance of recognizing this seminal event in Israel's history is underscored by the LORD's 1) repeating the commands regarding the Feast of Unleavened Bread, and 2) instituting another rite to be observed throughout the year.

The claim on every firstborn

> *1 Then the LORD spoke to Moses, saying, 2 "Sanctify to Me every firstborn, the first offspring of every womb among the sons of Israel, both of man and beast; it belongs to Me"* (13:1–2).

Back at the burning bush the LORD had instructed Moses to perform all the wonders which He would enable him to do. But even with such great displays of God's might, the king of Egypt would not be willing to consent to liberating the Jewish people. God told Moses to then say to Pharaoh, *"Thus says the LORD, 'Israel is My son, My firstborn. So I said to you, "Let My son go that he may serve Me"; but you have refused to let him go. Behold, I will kill your son, your firstborn'"* (4:22–23).

At the cost of the firstborn of Egypt, including his own son, Pharaoh relents and allows the Jewish people to leave his land. Having redeemed Abraham's descendants from bondage as promised (Genesis 15:13–14), God now lays claim to every firstborn male among the people and animals of Israel.

Remember this day

Moses is careful to pass along the information received from the LORD:

> *3 "Remember this day in which you went out from Egypt, from the house of slavery; for by a powerful hand the LORD brought you out from this place. And nothing leavened shall be eaten. 4 On this day in the month of Abib, you are about to go forth. 5 It shall be when the LORD brings you to the land of the Canaanite, the Hittite, the Amorite, the Hivite and the Jebusite, which He swore to your fathers to give you, a land flowing with milk and honey, that you shall observe this rite in this month"* (13:3–4).

This should sound familiar. Just as parents often remind their kids to "remember what's important," the lesson of Passover is a refrain the LORD continues to repeat. For generations to come, He will remind His people, *"I am the LORD your God who brought you out of Egypt."*

Celebration of Passover and eating unleavened bread in the appointed month was to be accompanied by recitation of the story. And not some dry account of ancient history, but a personal testimony of God's goodness:

> 8 *"You shall tell your son on that day, saying, 'It is because of what the LORD did for me when I came out of Egypt.' 9 And it shall serve as a sign to you on your hand, and as a reminder on your forehead, that the law of the LORD may be in your mouth; for with a powerful hand the LORD brought you out of Egypt. 10 Therefore, you shall keep this ordinance at its appointed time from year to year"* (13:8–10).

Redemption of the firstborn

God has another plan in mind to help His people value their redemption. When He brings the Jewish people to the land of Canaan and gives it to them as He covenanted to do, they will have an obligation to fulfill. The firstborn male offspring of man or beast is to be devoted to the LORD[1] (13:11–13).

---

1 In Numbers 18:15–18 we learn further details about *pidyon haben* (redemption of the firstborn). "Every devoted thing in Israel" would belong to the priests, including the firstborn males as follows:

- Clean animals (oxen, sheep, goats) were to be sacrificed; the meat was for the priests to eat.

And just as with Passover, there is a memorial purpose to this rite.

> *14 "And it shall be when your son asks you in time to come, saying, 'What is this?' then you shall say to him, 'With a powerful hand the LORD brought us out of Egypt, from the house of slavery. 15 It came about, when Pharaoh was stubborn about letting us go, that the LORD killed every firstborn in the land of Egypt, both the firstborn of man and the firstborn of beast. Therefore, I sacrifice to the LORD the males, the first offspring of every womb, but every firstborn of my sons I redeem.' 16 So it shall serve as a sign on your hand and as phylacteries on your forehead, for with a powerful hand the LORD brought us out of Egypt"* (13:14–16).

Fear factor/Misery index

George Santayana's statement "Those who do not remember history are condemned to repeat it" is often quoted because it rings true. The Creator "hardwired" memorials into Israel's calendar and life-cycle rituals to ensure His people would remember who their God is and what He has done for them. And then He reminds

---

• Baby boys and unclean animals (e.g., donkeys) were to be redeemed 30 days after birth by giving five silver shekels to the sanctuary (the wilderness tabernacle, then the temple when built in Jerusalem).

Today there is no temple, but the tradition of redeeming the firstborn son continues among observant Jewish families. On the 31st day after the first son's birth (unless it is a Sabbath), the father contributes five silver coins to a *cohen* (priestly descendant of Moses' brother, Aaron).

them to tell their children so they will pass along their godly heritage.

Moses is 80 years old when he experiences the Exodus. For the next 40 years he will shepherd the flock of Israel in the wilderness. At 120 he issues his last series of instructions to the second generation of the children of Israel. The book of Deuteronomy contains six "do not forget" reminders. Here's one: *Then watch yourself, that you do not forget the LORD who brought you from the land of Egypt, out of the house of slavery* (Deuteronomy 6:12).

Additionally, 14 times Moses exhorts the Jewish people to remember; the majority of those times it is their redemption from Egypt they must recall.

Moses also warned of the consequences of forgetting: *"It shall come about if you ever forget the LORD your God and go after other gods and serve them and worship them, I testify against you today that you will surely perish"* (Deuteronomy 8:19).

One of the sad realities of our fallen human condition is that we too quickly forget what the LORD has done for us. God intended the annual Passover to be one of those perpetual reminders of His sovereign goodness. But sometime after Israel's conquest of Canaan, observance of Passover would cease.[2]

---

2 We read in 2 Chronicles 34 of a young King Josiah who "rediscovers" the neglected treasure of God's Word. When the Torah is read to him, the king tears his clothes in repentance. *"Go, inquire of the LORD for me and for those who are left in Israel and in Judah, concerning the words of the book which has been found; for great is the wrath of the LORD which is poured out on us because our*

Where is God?

God delivers on His promise by delivering His people. He provides both celebrations and rites to help them remember.

The LORD still is worthy of the praises of His people. As you reflect on His redemptive grace and sovereign goodness in your life, why not thank Him, even in this moment? Take time to tell of His excellent greatness by relating a personal story to your children and grandchildren of God's guarding, guiding, and providing.

---

fathers have not observed the word of the LORD, to do according to all that is written in this book" (2 Chronicles 34:19–21).

Hearing the Torah is the first step; heeding the Lord's instructions is the next. The chronicler tells of a tremendous national celebration of the Jewish people's exodus from Egypt. *There had not been celebrated a Passover like it in Israel since the days of Samuel the prophet; nor had any of the kings of Israel celebrated such a Passover as Josiah did with the priests, the Levites, all Judah and Israel who were present, and the inhabitants of Jerusalem* (2 Chronicles 35:18).

Chapter 26
When Elation Turns to Fright

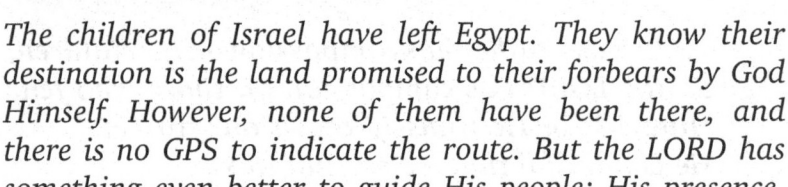

The children of Israel have left Egypt. They know their destination is the land promised to their forbears by God Himself. However, none of them have been there, and there is no GPS to indicate the route. But the LORD has something even better to guide His people: His presence. So, all will be well – right?

The tender heart of God

We have seen how often Moses includes insights into God's thoughts which reveal His character. So here:

> *17 Now when Pharaoh had let the people go, God did not lead them by the way of the land of the Philistines, even though it was near; for God said, "The people might change their minds when they see war, and return to Egypt." 18 Hence God led*

145

the people around by the way of the wilderness to the Red Sea (13:17–18).

The shortest route from Egypt to Canaan would have been what the Romans would later call the Via Maris, "the Way of the Sea," along the southeastern coast of the Mediterranean. The Philistines, who will play a significant role in centuries to come in Israel's history, were formidable fighters. Doubtless many of the Hebrews were in good physical shape from the rigors of their labors. But they were neither trained nor experienced in warfare as yet. Knowing this, the LORD plotted a more southern route, heading east for the Sinai Peninsula.

King David reflected on God's tender heart in Psalm 103:

> *13 Just as a father has compassion on his children, So the LORD has compassion on those who fear Him. 14 For He Himself knows our frame; He is mindful that we are but dust.*

Details, details

We learn *the sons of Israel went up in martial array from the land of Egypt* (13:18). As noted above, we have no indication the Hebrews were trained fighters. Moreover, in the list of the plunder donated by the Egyptians there is no mention of swords, spears, or other weapons of warfare. More likely the Hebrew term indicates this mass of people was already organized into manageable groups, moving forward in orderly form under Moses' leadership.

In another reference to the Genesis record, specifically where Joseph instructed the Jewish people regarding his remains, *Moses took the bones of Joseph with him* (13:19).

We have our first geographic markers along the exodus route. *Then they set out from Succoth and camped in Etham on the edge of the wilderness* (13:20).

Divine guidance

How often we have prayed for the LORD to show us the way along life's journey. If there ever is a time we desire the LORD's presence, protection, and guidance, it's when the path ahead seems uncertain or dangerous. That's exactly the situation faced by the Jewish people. And God is there for them!

> *21 The LORD was going before them in a pillar of cloud by day to lead them on the way, and in a pillar of fire by night to give them light, that they might travel by day and by night. 22 He did not take away the pillar of cloud by day, nor the pillar of fire by night, from before the people* (13:21–22).

The LORD continues to speak to Moses along the way as well. He gives both travel instructions (e.g., turn back, camp there) and informs of future actions – His own as well as Pharaoh's (14:1–4).

Back on the attack

> *5 When the king of Egypt was told that the people had fled, Pharaoh and his servants had a change of heart toward the people, and they said, "What is this we have done, that we have let Israel go from serving us?"* (14:5).

Here is another classic example of remorse rather than repentance. True heart repentance is evidenced by a lasting change of attitudes and behaviors. Pharaoh already had an established track record of making promises to have God remove His judgments, then reneging.[1]

Pharaoh and the Egyptians wake up to the realization their slave labor force is gone. We are not surprised at their response:

> *6 So [Pharaoh] made his chariot ready and took his people with him; 7 and he took six hundred select chariots, and all the other chariots of Egypt with officers over all of them. 8 The LORD hardened the heart of Pharaoh, king of Egypt, and he chased after the sons of Israel as the sons of Israel were going out boldly. 9 Then the Egyptians chased after them with all the horses and chariots of Pharaoh, his horsemen and his army, and they*

---

1 After the fourth plague (flies) Pharaoh bargained with Moses about the terms of the agreement to let the Jewish people have a "worship break." After the seventh and eight plagues (hail and locusts) Pharaoh admitted his sin and offered new terms to Moses, then did not follow through. Plague 9 (darkness) brought the most expansive offer, which was also retracted. Pharaoh wants his circumstances, not his heart, to change. How often is that true of us?

overtook them camping by the sea, beside Pi-hahiroth, in front of Baal-zephon (14:6–9).

A fearful response

God has demonstrated His power 10 times over. The children of Israel are now free – or thought they were. Someone checked the rearview mirror, saw Pharaoh's entire army, horses and chariots included, heading in their direction, and sounded the alarm. And a fearful alarm it was.

> *10 As Pharaoh drew near, the sons of Israel looked, and behold, the Egyptians were marching after them, and they became very frightened; so the sons of Israel cried out to the LORD* (14:10).

We're all familiar with the very human response when terror strikes. "Oh my God!!" or an equivalent seems to tumble from the lips of even hardened agnostics. Reasonable people will agree that a pursuing army is cause for real fear. The Jewish people had endured prolonged torment from the Egyptians. No one need inform them of the consequences when the powerful military again will have them in their grasp.

"Help us, LORD!!" is a prayer with which we can relate. Perhaps you can also relate to this:

> *11 Then they said to Moses, "Is it because there were no graves in Egypt that you have taken us away to die in the wilderness? Why have you dealt with us in this way, bringing us out*

> *of Egypt? 12 Is this not the word that we spoke*
> *to you in Egypt, saying, 'Leave us alone that we*
> *may serve the Egyptians'? For it would have been*
> *better for us to serve the Egyptians than to die in*
> *the wilderness"* (14:11–12).

Sarcasm can mask anger. No mask is needed here. This incident parallels the earlier chapters of Exodus. Times are tough. God's people cry out. No relief is in sight.

We saw when Moses showed up in Egypt with a word of encouragement ("We're getting out of here!") that initially hope sprang up. Then, in the first instance Pharaoh says, "Forget it – and work harder." And the spark of hope quickly goes out when circumstances worsen rather than improving.

But what about after witnessing the power of God unleashed in 10 plagues? Will trust in the LORD be evidenced? The Hebrews' very human response to a new and serious threat is, "Yeah, we escaped – and now we're dead."

Proverbs 13:12 states, *Hope deferred makes the heart sick, but desire fulfilled is a tree of life.* How much more difficult is it when deferred hope becomes a reality, but the "tree of life" is torn away before it has opportunity to take root?

Fear factor/Misery index

The thrill of escaping Egypt – at long last – is short-lived. The children of Israel "lifted up their eyes" and their hearts fell. The charging Egyptian army produced great fear. A fear grounded in the reality of a desperate situation. Unarmed fugitives stand no chance against chariots and armed horsemen skilled in battle. The situation faced by the Jewish people here epitomizes the expression "between the devil and the deep blue sea."

Let's face it: For many people, life is a roller coaster. Our emotions – including fear – rise and fall as our circumstances change. We cry out to God for rescue and relief, then despair when suffering is prolonged.

Where is God?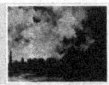

We have seen the LORD present in multiple ways in this passage.

- He is purposeful (and tender) in choosing the best route for His people.[2]
- He is *going before them in a pillar of cloud by day to lead them on the way, and in a pillar of fire by night to give them light* (13:21–22).
- He tells Moses in advance of Pharaoh's thoughts (14:3).
- He hardens Pharaoh's heart (14:4, 8).

What's more, He reveals His sovereign purpose in arranging for Pharaoh to come storming after the Jewish people: *"I will be honored through Pharaoh and all his army, and the Egyptians will know that I am the LORD"* (14:14).

---

2 Exodus 13:17–18; 14:2.

Perhaps the greatest lesson for us to remember is this: *God is purposeful in all that He does, and His purposes are always good – even when my circumstances are difficult.*

There is no end to which God will not go for the glory of His own name.[3] He puts His people in very vulnerable positions where massive foes mobilize against them. This includes whatever is threatening our safety, security, and comfort right now.

Do we consider that perhaps people around us who don't yet know the LORD may be drawn to Him when we respond to crises with humility, faith, and obedience? It is precisely in our overcoming the greatest challenges that God gets the greatest glory.

Think of how differently we would feel about:
Moses – if the Red Sea were a mere puddle to jump.

Joshua – if he kicked over a sandcastle at the beach rather than defeating a walled city.

David – if he bullied a little kid on the playground instead of slaying a giant foe.

Esther – if all she did was win a beauty pageant rather than risk her life for her people.

Daniel – if he played in his room with his tabby cat instead of facing down hungry lions.

No, we name our kids after these heroes of the faith because they confronted real foes, overcame tremendous

---

3 God's righteous character self-limits His actions, of course. In contrast to the sinful human heart which will justify any means to achieve a selfish end, God's purposes and actions are always pure.

odds, and acted boldly in the face of death because they trusted God.

It's human nature to want our struggles to cease. It's God's purpose to help us be victorious in them.

It's fine for us to acknowledge we're not up to the challenge. Our wisdom, experience, and resources are often insufficient for us to be confident of winning.

But for the believer it's not okay to doubt God's wisdom or sufficiency. His wisdom is rich, His judgments unsearchable, His ways unfathomable to mere humans (Romans 11:33–34). His strength is made perfect in our weakness (2 Corinthians 12:7–10). And success is measured by obedience for God's name's sake, not our personal security, comfort, or advancement.

Chapter 27

While You Keep Silent

Exodus 14:13–22

The Hebrew slaves have been freed. They marched in orderly fashion out of Goshen, following the pillar of cloud as God led them. Now at the edge of the Red Sea, their hearts fail them for fear. Pharaoh's military might is closing in – fast. Moses takes the brunt of their emotional outburst: "Better to serve the Egyptians than die in the desert!"

A leader in crisis

Leadership has its privileges – and its demands. Moses served as mediator between God and the people (Egyptian and Jewish) while the LORD poured out His judgments on the gods of Egypt and demonstrated His power to those oppressing His people. After the ninth plague we read, ***Moses himself was greatly esteemed in the land of Egypt, both in the sight of Pharaoh's servants and in the sight of the people*** (11:3).

Now faced with Pharaoh's pursuing army and hemmed in by the sea, the Hebrews confront Moses. "Why in the world did you bring us out to the wilderness just to die? We should have known better than to listen to you!"[1] (14:11–12).

The LORD had informed Moses He would harden Pharaoh's heart, so there should have been little surprise to see the Egyptian army advancing. But the array of military might bearing down on them would give anyone pause. How will Moses respond?

> *13 But Moses said to the people, "Do not fear! Stand by and see the salvation of the LORD which He will accomplish for you today; for the Egyptians whom you have seen today, you will never see them again forever. 14 The LORD will fight for you while you keep silent"* (14:13–14).

Get a move on!

Then the LORD said to Moses, "Why are you[2] crying out to Me? Tell the sons of Israel to go forward (14:15). There is a time to talk, and a time to act.

Once again Moses' trusty staff is to be lifted at God's command. That's Moses' responsibility. God's part is to harden Pharaoh's heart – for the fourth and final time (14:17–18).

---

1 Paraphrased.

2 Of note, God addresses Moses only: the "you" here is second person singular. Exodus 14:10 tells us "the sons of Israel cried out to the LORD" out of their fright. So why did God tell Moses to "quit yelling and get going"? The text doesn't tell us.

Security blanket and night light

How much does God care for His people? He knows what will calm the hearts of frightened folks and protect them. The angel of God and pillar of cloud which had been leading the way out of Egypt now reposition to become Israel's rear guard.

And since it was now night, the cloud also provided illumination – but only for the Jewish people. The pursuing Egyptians were literally left in the dark (14:19–20).

Through the midst of the sea

One of the most memorable of God's miracles is described with few details:

> *21 Then Moses stretched out his hand over the sea; and the LORD swept the sea back by a strong east wind all night and turned the sea into dry land, so the waters were divided. 22 The sons of Israel went through the midst of the sea on the dry land, and the waters were like a wall to them on their right hand and on their left* (14:21–22).

We haven't addressed some of the most debated elements of this story, such as the location of the sea.[3] The Scriptures provide some geographic markers: leaving from Succoth, camping in *"Etham on the edge of the wilderness"* (13:20); Pi-hahiroth and Baal-zephon

---

3 The "Red Sea" is actually the "Reed Sea" in Hebrew. But then again, the Red Sea is a brilliant blue, thus misnamed! (However, when the reddish mountains of Edom are reflected in a blazing Middle Eastern sunset ...)

(14:9). But we don't know with certainty where any of those places are today.

We also don't know how long it took for God to lead Israel *around by the way of the wilderness to the Red Sea* (13:18). If Pharaoh mobilized very quickly, the likely setting would be the Nile Delta region. Horses and chariots travel much faster than a multitude of families on foot. Over the millennia, the geography and topography have shifted considerably, so reconstructing what the "Reed Sea" looked like is only speculative.[4]

Naturalistic explanations for the parting of the sea abound. The text itself tells us that God used a strong wind to separate the waters – just as He employed real frogs, lice, hail, and locusts in the plagues.

What isn't so easy to explain is how the water parted in such a way as to form a wall on both the left and right sides. Simply moving the sea to one side (as explained by some to be the result of an earthquake) doesn't fit the scene as described in Scripture. And practically speaking, this many people[5] surely didn't move through a narrow pathway in the course of an hour.

The story is told of a university student who endured the withering attack of an atheistic professor who pronounced as foolishness any notion of the supernatural. "There is a

4 For one Nile Delta crossing explanation, see **bit.ly/red-sea-wp**. Among those touting the Gulf of Aqaba as the crossing site (and placing Mount Sinai in Arabia) are the makers of Patterns of Evidence (see **bit.ly/red-sea-miracle**).

5 Exodus 12:37–38 numbers the Hebrew men at 600,000, not counting women, children, and the "mixed multitude" of Egyptians (and others?) who formed the exiting multitude. For a reasoned consideration of the number, see **bit.ly/israelites-exited-egypt**.

scientific explanation for all the so-called miracles in the Bible. For instance, meteorologists have demonstrated that strong winds have dried up a pathway in the reedy marshes of the Nile where the Hebrews crossed. And by the way, the so-called 'sea' is only four inches deep," ridiculed the prof.

The student, a strong believer in God's Word, yelled out, "Praise God! What a miracle!"

The startled professor sneered, "Miracle! What miracle? I just explained this was a natural occurrence."

The student responded, "Then it was miraculous that Pharaoh's armies, horsemen, and chariots all drowned in four inches of water!" (But that's getting ahead of our almost-completed story.)

Fear factor/Misery index

"Don't be afraid!" How often have we said that to others? It's easy to comfort a child who fears a non-existent bogeyman. It's another thing to calm the heart of another when our own is racing in the face of a significant threat.

What does it mean when the LORD Himself says, "Do not fear"? The first occurrence of that phrase is recorded in Scripture when God appears to Abram (Genesis 15:1).[6]

---

6 Subsequently, the LORD (or the angel of God) will say "Do not be afraid" the next two times: to Hagar (Genesis 21:17) and Isaac (Genesis 26:24). Jacob also hears these words (Genesis 46:3).

Now Moses[7] seeks to calm a panicking people with those words. But his assurance is not based on his leadership skills or military prowess. The LORD will deliver His people, and without their assistance. Their assignment: keep still.

Where is God?

Psalm 91 is a favorite passage to which many turn when life overwhelms. It speaks specifically to our fears in times of danger:

> *5 You will not be afraid of the terror by night,*
> *Or of the arrow that flies by day;*
> *6 Of the pestilence that stalks in darkness,*
> *Or of the destruction that lays waste at noon.*

Among the reassurances the LORD gives are these words: *For He will give His angels charge concerning you, to guard you in all your ways* (Psalm 91:11).

Whether disguised or invisible to us, angelic beings are *all ministering spirits sent out to serve for the sake of those who are to inherit salvation* (Hebrews 1:11–14). Since the psalmist tells us they "guard you in all your ways," we ought not to think they only show up for emergencies but are continually[8] on watch.

---

7 The only other time Moses tells Israel not to fear is when the LORD appears on Mount Sinai with thunder and lightning, trumpets and smoke (20:18–20).

8 Well, perhaps not in my case. I likely wore out more than a few guardian angels. According to my godly grandmother, "The angels step out of the car when you drive over 60 miles per hour."

Where is God in fearful times? On watch, always. *Behold, He who keeps Israel will neither slumber nor sleep* (Psalm 121:4).

Chapter 28
The LORD Fights for Israel

Exodus 14:23–31

"It was simply amazing!! All night we walked through the midst of the sea on dry land, the LORD lighting our path. On our right hand, a wall of water. On the left, another wall. And you won't believe what happened next!"

All the king's horses and all the king's men

The Egyptian soldiers had been separated from the Israelite camp, obscured by the cloud (14:19–20). All during the night the LORD sent a strong east wind to open an escape route for Israel (14:21–22).

At some point the pursuers discovered their quarry had moved. Our narrator doesn't record their stunned response to this unbelievable stealth maneuver of the Hebrews. Since when does a path open in a sea?

We are told about the army's actions. *Then the Egyptians took up the pursuit, and all Pharaoh's horses, his chariots and his horsemen went in after them into the midst of the sea*[1] (14:23).

Divine intervention

During the small hours of the morning,[2] the LORD has a look at what's transpiring. Through the pillar of fire and cloud He sees the advancing Egyptian forces. He *brought the army of the Egyptians into confusion. 25 He caused their chariot wheels to swerve, and He made them drive with difficulty* (14:24–25).

Given the military's imminent demise, one may wonder why the Almighty takes this final opportunity to demonstrate His sovereign control over earthly events. Our clue is found in the military's response: *"Let us flee from Israel, for the LORD is fighting for them against the Egyptians"* (14:25).

A warrior trained for battle has no concern when pursuing unarmed slaves on the run. Victory is assured with no casualties expected. But losing control of chariots while surrounded by walls of water amidst the Red Sea was not something for which they had trained. Mid-charge, the Egyptians discover this is not an enterprise worth pursuing. More than simply giving up the chase, they sense the need to flee for their lives.

---

1 We may glean from this that the children of Israel were still in the process of moving that great mass of people through the Red Sea.

2 The morning watch is from 2 a.m. until dawn.

God had promised He would *"be honored through Pharaoh and all his army, through his chariots and his horsemen. 18 Then the Egyptians will know that I am the LORD, when I am honored through Pharaoh, through his chariots and his horsemen"* (14:17–18). In this very last moment, Pharaoh's troops knew the reality that *"the LORD, He is God."*[3]

Not even one remained

Once more Moses, now safely across the Red Sea, is instructed to stretch out his hand over the waters. He does so,

> *...and the sea returned to its normal state at daybreak, while the Egyptians were fleeing right into it; then the LORD overthrew the Egyptians in the midst of the sea. 28 The waters returned and covered the chariots and the horsemen, even Pharaoh's entire army that had gone into the sea after them; not even one of them remained* (14:27–28).

The first nine plagues had brought devastating losses to Egypt's possessions. Following the tenth, the people mourned the death of their firstborn. Now the powerful Egyptian army, which had gone to retrieve their escaped

---

3 This is the repeated phrase of the Jewish people following another demonstration of the LORD's superiority over a pagan deity. God rained fire from heaven when Elijah prayed, *"O LORD, the God of Abraham, Isaac and Israel, today let it be known that You are God in Israel and that I am Your servant and I have done all these things at Your word. 37 Answer me, O LORD, answer me, that this people may know that You, O LORD, are God, and that You have turned their heart back again"* (1 Kings 18:36c–37). The showdown on Mount Carmel resulted in victory over Baal and the priests who served him.

labor force to rebuild their shattered economy, is eliminated in a moment.

Fear factor/Misery index

How swiftly life's circumstances can change. Pharaoh's forces went from conquerors to confounded to consumed in a matter of minutes. The Jewish people, whose hearts were failing them for fear when the Egyptian army appeared, have seen God's overnight deliverance in a most remarkable way.

Where is God?

Skeptics will doubt, scoffers will mock, and brilliant minds lacking wisdom will seek alternate explanations for "coincidences." But our text is clear: ***Thus the LORD saved Israel that day from the hand of the Egyptians, and Israel saw the Egyptians dead on the seashore*** (14:30).

> ***"For the LORD is fighting for you"*** is a theme that will be repeated in Israel's history.

> ***"Do not fear them, for the LORD your God is the one fighting for you"*** (Deuteronomy 3:22).

> ***"... for the LORD your God is the one who goes with you, to fight for you against your enemies, to save you"*** (Deuteronomy 20:4).

"One of your men puts to flight a thousand, for the LORD your God is He who fights for you, just as He promised you" (Joshua 23:10).

What is an appropriate response to God's deliverance of His people and destruction of their enemies?

When Israel saw the great power which the LORD had used against the Egyptians, the people feared the LORD, and they believed in the LORD and in His servant Moses (14:31).

The "fear of the LORD" is the best kind of fear. It produces what God designed and desires us to do: honor Him for Who He is and glorify Him for His awesome deeds.

For the first time we read that Israel *"believed in the LORD and in His servant Moses."* And as we shall see in the final study in this series, their faith resulted in worship.

Personal application

How is your "fear of the LORD" producing faith and worship in the midst of these fearful times? It's easy to believe God is good when our health is good, our relationships are strong, our country is at peace, and our finances are in order.

But even should "all the stars align" and our circumstances are as we would desire, we recognize the transitory nature of life[4] in our fallen world. The challenge is, how do we respond amidst adversity?

Habakkuk takes an accurate inventory in his day and comes up short in every category. But check out the lyrics to the song he composes:

> *17 Though the fig tree should not blossom*
> *And there be no fruit on the vines,*
> *Though the yield of the olive should fail*
> *And the fields produce no food,*
> *Though the flock should be cut off from the fold*
> *And there be no cattle in the stalls,*
> *18 Yet I will exult in the LORD,*
> *I will rejoice in the God of my salvation.*
> *19 The Lord GOD is my strength,*
> *And He has made my feet like hinds' feet,*
> *And makes me walk on my high places.*
> *For the choir director, on my stringed instruments*
> (Habakkuk 3:17–19).

What song would you sing to the LORD in your present circumstances?

---

4 Our days pass "swifter than a weaver's shuttle" (Job 7:6), "as a shadow" (Job 8:9), "swifter than a runner" (Job 9:25), as "a wind that passes" (Psalm 78:39), "like grass ... a flower of the field" (Psalm 103:15), "like a mere breath" (Psalm 144:4), and "a vapor that appears for a little while, and then vanishes away" (James 4:14).

Chapter 29

Great Things He Has Done

Exodus 15:1–21

We've traced Moses' story through the phases of his life: preserved infant, prince, shepherd, ambassador of the LORD in Pharaoh's throne room, and leader of a nation. Now we discover Moses as poet. Here we see Israel's original "shepherd-songwriter" – a role King David later will make famous.

The Song of Moses

We don't have the melody, but the lyrics sung by Moses and the people of Israel have been preserved in Exodus 15:

> *"I will sing to the LORD, for He is highly exalted;*
> *The horse and its rider He has hurled into the sea.*

2 The LORD is my strength and song, And He has become my salvation; This is my God, and I will praise Him; My father's God, and I will extol Him.
3 The LORD is a warrior; The LORD is His name.
4 Pharaoh's chariots and his army He has cast into the sea; And the choicest of his officers are drowned in the Red Sea.
5 The deeps cover them; They went down into the depths like a stone.
6 Your right hand, O LORD, is majestic in power, Your right hand, O LORD, shatters the enemy.
7 And in the greatness of Your excellence You overthrow those who rise up against You; You send forth Your burning anger, and it consumes them as chaff.
8 At the blast of Your nostrils the waters were piled up, The flowing waters stood up like a heap; The deeps were congealed in the heart of the sea.
9 The enemy said, 'I will pursue, I will overtake, I will divide the spoil; My desire shall be gratified against them; I will draw out my sword, my hand will destroy them.'
10 You blew with Your wind, the sea covered them; They sank like lead in the mighty waters.
11 Who is like You among the gods, O LORD? Who is like You, majestic in holiness, Awesome in praises, working wonders?
12 You stretched out Your right hand, The earth swallowed them.
13 In Your lovingkindness You have led the people whom You have redeemed; In Your strength You have guided them to Your holy habitation.

14 The peoples have heard, they tremble; Anguish has gripped the inhabitants of Philistia.

15 Then the chiefs of Edom were dismayed; The leaders of Moab, trembling grips them; All the inhabitants of Canaan have melted away.

16 Terror and dread fall upon them; By the greatness of Your arm they are motionless as stone; Until Your people pass over, O LORD, Until the people pass over whom You have purchased.

17 You will bring them and plant them in the mountain of Your inheritance, The place, O LORD, which You have made for Your dwelling, The sanctuary, O LORD, which Your hands have established.

18 The LORD shall reign forever and ever."

A personal testimony

Moses begins his song in the first-person singular: *I will sing* (15:1a). Yes, others may sing along, but for Moses this is a personal testimony.

Moses is singing *to the LORD, for He is highly exalted* (15:1b). The LORD is Moses' strength, song, and salvation. His father's God is his God, and Moses is bent on praising and extoling Him (15:2).

The victory in poetry

Moses first references the historical event he had just witnessed by highlighting a single snapshot of what transpired. *The horse and its rider He has hurled into the sea* (15:1d). Battle scenes are interspersed with praises throughout his composition. Here are his descriptions in verse of Pharaoh's forces and their demise:

- The enemy's stated intent is to pursue, plunder, and destroy Israel with the sword (15:9).

- Pharaoh's chariots and army, including his best officers, drown like stones, like lead in the depths of the sea.[1]

Moses leaves no doubt as to the identity of the hero of his epic song: the God of Israel. Moses depicts Him with vivid brushstrokes:

- The LORD is a warrior (15:3).

- His right hand is **majestic in power**, overthrowing and shattering His foes in the greatness of His excellence, consuming them in His wrath (15:6–7).

- The gale that divided the waters is a **blast from God's nostrils**; His wind also closed up the mighty waters.[2]

- The rhetorical question, **Who is like You among the gods, O LORD?**[3] anticipates a "No one!" in response. **Majestic in holiness, awesome in praises, working wonders** (15:11) can only describe the Creator of the Universe.

---

1 Exodus 15:4–5, 10c.

2 Exodus 15:8, 10a.

3 This verse in Hebrew begins *Mi chamocha*. These words have been recited as a traditional Sabbath prayer in synagogues around the world for centuries, acknowledging the uniqueness and superiority of the God of Israel. Moses later will underscore this to the children of the exodus generation in Deuteronomy 4:32–39.

We have a shift to the prophetic future beginning in verse 13. Moses references God's lovingkindness in leading His redeemed people *to Your holy habitation* (15:13). Obviously, the other side of the Red Sea is not yet that place, but the people of God are on their way to the land promised to Abraham. Verse 17 speaks of *the mountain of Your inheritance* as the place God will plant the Jewish people, where the sanctuary for His dwelling[4] will be (15:17).

There is also mention of how the neighboring nations will respond when the news reaches them of how Israel's God has fought for them. Philistia, Moab, and Canaan are specifically named. They will tremble in anguish, dismay, terror, and dread,[5] becoming "motionless as stone" (15:14–16). Note this will continue until[6] the Jewish people pass through to the place God is leading them: the Promised Land. Moses is not only a poet but also a prophet.

All together now

"They drowned, we didn't even get our feet wet" is provided as a summary recap (15:19).[7] Then Moses'

---

4 Moses is speaking of Jerusalem; compare Deuteronomy 12:5 (the place which the LORD your God will choose from all your tribes, to establish His name there for His dwelling) with the LORD's statement in 2 Chronicles 6:6 ("but I have chosen Jerusalem that My name might be there").

5 As an example of how this was fulfilled, consider Rahab's testimony in Jericho (Joshua 2:9–11).

6 At the time he composed the song, Moses had no clue that 40 years would pass before the children of Israel will enter the Land, nor that he would not accompany them across the Jordan River.

7 Paraphrased.

sister Miriam[8] leads the women, dancing and playing timbrels, in the chorus:

> *"Sing to the LORD, for He is highly exalted;*
> *The horse and his rider He has hurled into the*
> *sea"* (15:21).

Fear factor/Misery index

Their fear dissipated, the misery of bondage ended, the Jewish people have reason to rejoice. Yes, there is song and dance, but it begins and ends with *Sing to the LORD*. True, the enemy has been not only defeated but destroyed. But Moses ensures Israel's focus will be vertical as he exalts the One who brought the victory.

Where is God?

As we close our study (with only an epilogue to follow), we find God exactly where He should be: honored, extolled, and worshiped by a grateful people recounting His righteous deeds, majestic power, and excellent greatness.

A fitting conclusion

Moses ends his song of praise to the LORD with these words: *"The LORD shall reign forever and ever"* (15:18). These words, evoking the stirring conclusion of Handel's magnificent *Messiah*, echo Isaiah 9:6–7:

---

8 This is the first time the text names Moses' sister. Miriam is identified here as a prophetess, also the first use of the word.

6 For a child will be born to us, a son will be given to us; And the government will rest on His shoulders; And His name will be called Wonderful Counselor, Mighty God, Eternal Father, Prince of Peace.

7 There will be no end to the increase of His government or of peace, On the throne of David and over his kingdom, To establish it and to uphold it with justice and righteousness From then on and forevermore. The zeal of the LORD of hosts will accomplish this.

The reminder of God's eternal dominion and Messiah's "forevermore rule" should be an energizing encouragement to us today. No matter how difficult our present circumstances, our powerlessness to control them, or our uncertainty about tomorrow, we can take comfort in the reality that our "know for certain" God[9] has written a script with a wonderful ending.

When you rewatch a favorite movie or replay a sporting event, you may get caught up in the drama. But when you've seen it before, you know "the good guys win in the end."

We all experience life in real time, right now. But God has already written the final chapter. He wins. And when we're on His side, we win, too.

---

9 God's words to Abram in Genesis 15:13 telling of the 400 years of enslavement and oppression before His redemption of Abram's descendants begin "Know for certain ..."

176 Where Is God in Fearful Times?

Chapter 30

Encouragement from Exodus
Epilogue

Where we've been

We began our study in Exodus during the dark days of oppression of the Hebrew people. The baby boys were under a death sentence. Shiphrah and Puah shone as lights in the darkness. These midwives feared the LORD and defied the king's orders.

We watched as God not only preserved the life of the infant Moses but saw to it that a slave child grew up with all the benefits of an Egyptian prince. At 40 Moses fled to Midian, learning to tend flocks in the wilderness, preparing him for another 40 years of shepherding the flock of Israel in the wilderness.

At 80 years of age Moses had a dramatic career change: "to be as God to Pharaoh." Moses heard the voice of the LORD calling to him from the blazing bush which was not consumed. God deputized the reticent shepherd to represent Him: first to the Hebrew people, then to the Egyptians, and especially Pharaoh, the most powerful ruler of his generation. Aaron filled the role of spokesman, but Moses was the LORD's primary representative.

"That you may know ..."

When Pharaoh said, "I do not know the LORD," God said, "You will." And not only would Egypt's king and people learn who the God of Israel is, the Jewish people also had repeated opportunities to see His power on display for their benefit. Ten powerful plagues were unleashed on the Egyptians as the LORD executed His judgments against the gods of Egypt (12:12).

The God who says 14 times in Exodus *"That you may know that I am the LORD"* did not demonstrate His sovereign might for that generation alone. It will be the children of those redeemed from Egyptian bondage who will conquer Canaan. Moses will continue to remind them of what the LORD had done for their fathers.

Indeed, God will continue to state, *"I am the Lord your God who brought you up out of the land of Egypt."*[1] Multiple times Israel's prophets will also mention God's deliverance of the Jewish people, underscoring the singular importance of the exodus event in history.[2]

1 Nine times in the Torah (Exodus 6:7; 20:2; Leviticus 19:36; 22:33; 25:38; 25:55; 26:13; Numbers 15:41; Deuteronomy 5:6) and once in Judges 6:8, God identifies Himself to the Jewish people as the One who brought them out of Egypt.

2 Moses references this reality in pleading to God not to destroy His people in Exodus 32:11 (see also Deuteronomy 9:26) and exhorting them not to forget the LORD (Deuteronomy 6:12, 8:14), be seduced away from Him (Deuteronomy 13:10), or be fearful in battle (Deuteronomy 20:1). Samuel in his address to Israel

Notably, God's demonstration of His power over the Egyptians resulted in many of them exiting their homeland (12:38) to join the Hebrews headed for the Promised Land. And the epic saga of Israel's deliverance had an enduring impact on the nations of the Middle East. A generation after Pharaoh's army drowned, the Hebrew spies sent to scout Jericho heard Rahab say, *"For we have heard how the LORD dried up the water of the Red Sea before you when you came out of Egypt"*[3] (Joshua 2:10).

The LORD is a missionary God. He still wants to be known. In fact, His efforts to redeem His people extend far beyond displaying His power over false gods. "A prophet like Moses" was promised (Deuteronomy 18:15–18). God sent many prophets to speak to Israel (and famously, Jonah to preach to Nineveh). The narrator of the Torah closes with these words in Deuteronomy 34:

> *10 Since that time no prophet has risen in Israel like Moses, whom the LORD knew face to face, 11 for all the signs and wonders which the LORD sent him to perform in the land of Egypt against Pharaoh, all his servants, and all his land, 12 and for all the mighty power and for all the great terror which Moses performed in the sight of all Israel.*

---

before installing Saul as their first monarch (1 Samuel 12:8) and Daniel in his intercessory prayer on Israel's behalf (Daniel 9:15) also cite God's deliverance of the Jewish people from Egypt. (See also 2 Kings 17:36.)

3 See also the testimony of the Gibeonites in Joshua 9:9–10.

One greater than Moses

However, in the Messiah, whose coming was predicted by the prophets, we discover *"one greater than Moses"* (Hebrews 3:1–6). God's love for fallen humanity was demonstrated to the greatest extent in His provision of atonement for our sin through Messiah Yeshua (Jesus of Nazareth).[4]

Do you know Him? If not, please consider the words of Moses to Israel before his death. *But from there you will seek the LORD your God, and you will find Him if you search for Him with all your heart and all your soul* (Deuteronomy 4:29).

The pages of **InSearchofShalom.com** will point you to the promised Messiah who indeed "has also become our salvation." We are happy to assist in your search if you choose to chat, message, or call us.

If you do have a personal relationship with the living LORD, are you learning to abide in Messiah (John 15) and walk in the Spirit (Romans 8)? Check out the three-part "Navigating This Life" series on the TŌV Podcast, which begins with **lifeinmessiah.org/thetovpodcast/navigating-this-life.**

4 See Isaiah 53; John 3:16; Romans 5:5–21.

How are you doing in "making God famous"? If we can encourage you in living out and sharing your faith in a way that brings glory to God and draws others to Him, we'd be delighted to do so.

Who is Life in Messiah?

Since 1887, Life in Messiah has helped believers understand the Jewish roots of our faith and God's ongoing commitment to His people. In all we do, our priority is to share the gospel message.

Today, Life in Messiah has ministry to Jewish people in Israel, France, the Netherlands, Hong Kong, Argentina, Mexico, Canada, and the United States. Our continuing desire is to "share God's heart for the Jewish people" as we proclaim the Good News of Messiah, disciple believers to maturity, and train believers to reach their Jewish friends for the Savior.

We believe God is radically transforming Jewish people through the faithful obedience, prayer, and persistent love of believers around the world. Life in Messiah's humble role in this great evangelistic work is to develop teams, utilize technology, and equip the church, all with a priority "to the Jew first."

To learn more about our ministry, visit **lifeinmessiah.org.** We hope you will find encouragement from *The TŌV Podcast*, blogs, and stories from the field in our bi-annual publication, *The Bridge.* You will also find a wide variety of resources and practical ways to get involved.

Keep Learning

To learn more about Jewish evangelism, Jewish culture and history, or standing against antisemitism, visit **lifeinmessiah.org/resources**. There you will find a curated list of webpages, books, and videos to help you dive deeper into these important topics.

You can also scan the QR code below to access this resource.

If this book has been an encouragement to you, please pass it on to someone else or consider making a donation at **lifeinmessiah.org/donate**.